PRAISE FOR
GRACEFUL WOMAN WARRIOR

"The prospect of death concentrates the mind wonderfully. We listen to the words of those who know themselves to be dying, because they have a sharpened perception we won't have until it is our time. I listened very carefully to my wife Jeanne for all our 35 years—I found it profitable—but never so closely as after she was diagnosed with cancer. The same became true of our remarkable daughter Terri Luanna when her diagnosis arrived a year later. She was born with her mother's extraordinary wisdom, and since it was the last helping I would ever be offered, I worked hard at not missing a bite.

I believe you will find that her wisdom helps you as much as it helped me when I really needed it. I often summon up memories of her talking, so that I won't forget the sound of her voice—and when I do, the sentence she always seems to be saying is the one she said to me so often in her last year: 'It is what it is, Dad.' I think she got that from her mother, who was, in addition to a dancer, author, and musician, a Soto Zen priest. If anyone can help you with mere words, Terri Luanna will."

—Spider Robinson, co-author with Jeanne Robinson of *The Stardance Trilogy*

"Riding the cancer treatment roller coaster of hope to despair over and over again, the lessons Terri Luanna da Silva learned as she journeyed through cancer and ultimately death, are just what 'the doctor ordered'—to live your best possible life. Give yourself the gift of *Graceful Woman Warrior*."

—Christa Johnson, MD, Hospice and Palliative Care/Mind Body Medicine, author of *Lynn's Legacy, Mind, Body and Spirit*

"*Graceful Woman Warrior* is an incredible and inspiring story about one amazing woman's battle with cancer. As I read it, I was thinking, I would love to have met Terri Luanna and gotten to know her—until I realized that's exactly what was happening. I was both honored and humbled to tag along on Terri's courageous journey. And I am equally grateful for the wisdom she was generous enough to impart. I predict that *Graceful Woman Warrior* will impact countless souls. Be sure that you're one of those fortunate folks who give it a read!"

—Steve Manchester, author of *The Rocking Chair and Twelve Months*

For

Marisa Alegria Maitreya Robinson da Silva,

my greatest teacher.

You are just what I dreamed my daughter would be.

And so much more…

Love, Mamãe

"Shared pain is lessened; shared joy, increased."
—Spider Robinson

Callahan's Crosstime Saloon

CONTENTS

GRACEFUL
WOMAN
WARRIOR

FOREWORD

*"Stories are the creative conversion of life itself into a
more powerful, clearer, more meaningful experience.
They are the currency of human contact."*
-ROBERT MCKEE

S tories…

Everyone has a story.

But there are certain stories that must be told—stories that inspire, stories that enlighten, stories that break open your heart—and once opened, stories that offer answers to the profound and eternal questions humankind has been asking since the beginning of time. This is one such story.

Graceful Woman Warrior is a gutsy, thought-provoking and heart-rending memoir about mindfully living and dying with cancer. Forced to take an honest look at her own mortality after a Stage 4 breast cancer diagnosis, my 37-year-old niece, Terri Luanna da Silva, started a blog about her journey. Reeling from the recent death of her mother—visionary Canadian artist, Jeanne Robinson—Terri asked the big questions as she searched to understand the lessons contained within the pain and suffering of a terminal illness.

Compelled to use her diagnosis as an opportunity to grow, learn and discover who she truly was, thousands upon thousands of people were drawn to her riveting and illuminating story. Terri's blog offered a life perspective so rare, so powerfully transformative, so hopeful in the face of interminable darkness, it left a deep imprint on the hearts of each and every person who read it.

This book is a culmination of a promise I made to Terri when she whispered to me, "I think I'm dying. I want you to tell people." Through her bracing and open-hearted writing, Terri offers each of us the chance to awaken to our own lives—to tap into a newfound capacity to dig deeper and to live and love more vividly, more fully, more fearlessly and more intently.

But wait, I have to warn you. You must "prepare" for the journey ahead…

What should you bring?

Trust—that the Universe chose you to read *this* book, at *this* time in your life, to contemplate *these* lessons.

Faith—that like Terri, you too can uncover the gifts and lessons contained in life's toughest moments, and in so doing, conjure and create the life you envision.

And finally, courage—to bear witness to this bold, evocative, powerfully poignant exploration of the journey between, through and beyond life and death.

So I invite you to open your heart to Terri's haunting yet ultimately transcendent story with the full knowledge that in so doing, you are opening your heart to the possibility of reshaping, redefining or perhaps even rewriting the meaning of your own.

Laurie O'Neil
(Terri's Auntie L)

INTRODUCTION

On Dec 27, 2011, at 11:03 pm, Terri wrote the following email to her closest family and friends:

Hi all,

So I finally got my blog set up and wrote my first entry based on the crazy news I received from my oncologist today. I've done this because it's all part of my master plan to use my diagnosis as a platform to further my social work training and help people in a more public way.

The name of the site is www.gracefulwomanwarrior.com, in honor of my mom and the name she gave me, Luanna Mountainborn Robinson. Luanna means Graceful Woman Warrior. And it just happens to apply so perfectly to my breast cancer battle. My goal is to share all the love I receive with the rest of the world through my actions and through my words. If my blog puts a smile on someone's face or gives somebody something new to think about or offers a reminder about the lessons we all so easily forget in the daily madness, then I feel I'm working towards my goal.

Big hugs to everyone. And thanks for your continued support. Keep praying for me. I need all the positive healing energy I can get!

xoxo - Terri Luanna

PART 1

"GOD (OR BUDDHA, OR THE UNIVERSE, OR WHOMEVER) GRANT ME THE SERENITY TO ACCEPT THE THINGS I CANNOT CHANGE..."

CHAPTER 1

WTF?!

DECEMBER 29, 2011

Reality is sinking in… I have Stage 4 cancer.

It doesn't matter that I'm only 37-years-old. Or that I have a two-year-old daughter and husband who need me. Or that I was just reaching the prime of my life—finally ready to pursue my career as a social worker, filling out applications to become a foster parent and settling into a new and promising life in Ohio after two years of personal hell. No, none of that matters.

The reality is that I have metastatic breast cancer. The reality is that life is unfair.

To be honest, I'm a little confused about the whole situation. What started out as simple, easy, curable, Stage 2B breast cancer only a month ago, now appears to be Stage 4 metastatic breast cancer. It seems the PET scan I had last week shows some serious lymph node involvement beyond what we originally thought—positive lymph nodes around the chest muscles of both breasts, my lungs, collarbone, throat and other areas. Plus, there are some questionable areas in the bone marrow of my middle back and left leg femur bone—even though my bone scan from two weeks earlier said all my bones looked fine. As the title of this chapter says…WTF!?

This means my entire treatment protocol is changing. *To what?* We're still not sure yet.

I'm finding out about a bunch of possible clinical trials, going for an MRI to check on the status of the bone marrow concerns, consulting with my team at Sloan Kettering in NYC about the changes and revised diagnosis to see what they suggest and I'm planning to move my ENTIRE treatment over to a more respected and cutting-edge cancer center associated with Ohio State University in Columbus.

In the meantime, I was scheduled to start chemo on Thursday morning but tonight opted not to so I can leave all my options open for possible clinical trials (some of them won't accept you if you've had prior treatment). Regardless of whether I end up pursuing traditional treatment or a new clinical trial, I HAVE TO start doing something. I can't give those cancer cells any more time to stake claim to my body.

Emotionally, I'm a bit all over the place. I find myself looking around in stores and on the streets thinking, *Why don't all these overweight, unstable and unhealthy people have cancer? What the heck did I do that brought me to this point?* I'm upset I didn't trust my gut and seek treatment from a bigger hospital in a bigger city from the beginning. I'm pissed that I can never seem to get the full story about what's going on. I'm sick of all the tests, scans and doctors' appointments that have consumed my life every day. I'm pissed that this happened right after I moved to a new state where I know nobody and all my friends and family live in cities far away. I'm worried about my daughter and how this is all going to impact her. I'm scared.

For the first time since finding this out my husband and I acknowledged our new reality. Lying beside each other, we expressed our anger and sadness as well as our hope and belief that we can make it through this. I want to grow old with this man, raise a household of kids with this man, retire on a beach in Brazil with this man. It's hard for me to even fathom that might not be an option anymore.

My doctor in NYC says I can live with this. I will never be "cured." But it is possible to shrink down and eliminate enough cancer cells so that I can continue to live. *For how long?*

No one can say. All I can do is live in the moment and hope for the best.

Oddly enough, somewhere deep down inside of me a little voice keeps saying that I'm going to win this battle. Whatever "win" means is, of course, subject to interpretation.

Hopefully writing this blog will help on a number of levels—help me to express what I'm feeling and going through and help my loved ones stay up-to-date with what's going on.

And maybe it will even help another breast cancer warrior out there who happens to stumble across my blog and find something that resonates or touches them in some way. Welcome to my world.

CHAPTER 2

THE STATS

DECEMBER 30, 2011 (4:39 AM)

I've been avoiding reading anything about Stage 4 metastatic breast cancer for fear of what I'll see. But in preparation for my appointment in Columbus tomorrow I felt the need to do a little research. So online I went.

The good thing is that when you have late stage cancer a million more treatment options are available. Very promising drugs that are still in testing and trial mode for earlier stage cancers are practically standard treatment for us folks at the end of the line. Of course, this is because everyone figures when you're at the end of the line what have you got to lose?

What I'd been really avoiding was looking at the numbers—the survival statistics for Stage 4 and metastatic breast cancers. The numbers aren't pretty. Apparently only 15% of us survive longer than five years. On the flip side, I keep hearing stories about Stage 4 survivors that have gone on to live way longer than that. All I can say is that I plan on being one of the 15% that keeps on living.

On Monday I go for an MRI to find out more about the suspicious bone marrow situation—keeping my fingers crossed that the cancer hasn't spread to my bones. I have high hopes for my new medical team in Columbus and I'm anxious to finally get some answers and start my damn treatment already—and kick these cancer cells to the curb!

CHAPTER 3

RIDING THE ROLLER COASTER

DECEMBER 30, 2011 (10:17 PM)

The more doctors I meet with, the more confused I get.

There are just so many variables to consider—my relationship with the doctor, the reputation of the facility, the different treatment recommendations, access to cutting edge treatments, logistics and timing. How do I prioritize?

I went into my meeting in Columbus settled and sure in my plan to pursue treatment there, but I left feeling unsupported and unsure of my decision. While I loved the facility in all its sparkling glory, fancy amenities and resources, I did not love my doctor. Meanwhile, I really like the local small-town oncologist I've been working with but am very dubious about the local hospital. And while I loved everything about my experience in NYC, I just can't find a way to make pursuing treatment there a viable option. *Sigh.*

There really are no easy answers, are there?

What I do know is that I need to make a decision fast. My tumors have almost doubled in size since my initial diagnosis in mid-November. I need to start treatment now. I don't have time to keep shopping for the perfect doctor and treatment facility. I need to just make a decision and do something.

The emotional roller coaster of this diagnosis is so intense and psychotic. I started today confident and assured of my new plan, spent my drive home in a teary anger-filled rant of despair, sadness and confusion and then received a positive boost of hope and reassurance from stories of survival posted on the internet and shared by a dear family friend who is battling breast cancer herself.

And through it all, life goes on. The dishes need to be done. Toys need tidying. My little girl needs a bath and a bedtime story. Life goes on. And I will go on—just as thousands of other Stage 4 breast cancer warriors do.

CHAPTER 4

PRIORITY #1

JANUARY 2, 2012

A new year is upon us... 2012.

Hubby and I are trying to rid ourselves of any negative energy from 2011 and make space for new beginnings, hope and positivity. What are my specific goals and intentions for 2012? This is something I've been pondering since my diagnosis. I think it all comes down to self-care—looking out for #1 (as my home girls and I like to say).

For the last three years my life has been consumed by taking care of everyone but me. Through it all, everyone kept saying, "What are you doing for yourself? Make sure to take care of you..." But I honestly couldn't figure out how to do it amongst the insanity of moving a half dozen times, being essentially homeless for six months, taking care of my terminally-ill mom, my new baby, a depressed husband and organizing all my parents' affairs. I put myself on the back burner for too long. Now I see this breast cancer diagnosis as a big slap in the face reminder to put myself first.

So 2012 is all about taking care of me—exercise, meditation, eating well, therapy, quality time with those I love, doing things that bring me joy, dancing, being in nature, taking regular trips to NYC... And in taking care of myself, I will go on to live many more years and be an even better parent, wife, friend, daughter and human being.

In terms of treatment decisions—taking a couple of days to just sit with my options and talk it through with family helped immensely. I have decided to go with my local oncologist. I just like his vibe and feel that he's behind me in my vision to kick this cancer's ass (versus the Columbus team who made me feel like the cancer was going to kick my ass). And as my NYC doctor said, "Chemo is chemo." It doesn't matter if I'm getting it in a posh room in Manhattan or a simple office in Ohio—the process is the same.

So tomorrow is the big day. My first chemo session. I'll be taking three drugs (Herceptin, Taxol, and Carboplatin). They say it'll take around five-to-six hours to pump it all into my body.

Wishing everyone a Happy New Year and reminding you to make your own self-care a priority. NOW. Before life slaps you in the face.

CHAPTER 5

CHEMO QUEEN

JANUARY 3, 2012

I made it through my first day of chemo. Yay!

I took this picture before I left for my appointment—me in fighting stance, ready to kick some cancer ass! I woke up early, did 30 minutes on the elliptical machine, a 15-minute meditation, ate a healthy breakfast and I was ready and raring to go.

Luckily, I got a call last night from a special woman whom I now consider to be one of my breast cancer mentors. She prepped me for my visit today and let me know exactly what to expect.

But even that didn't fully prepare me for the reactions my body went through. I was convinced I wouldn't feel a thing. But it's kinda like when you have a baby and everyone warns you ahead of time about how intense it's going to be and you're like, *Yeah, yeah... I got this.* And then the baby comes and you're thrown into sleep-deprived insanity and you realize nothing anyone could have said would have prepared you for this.

First, let me say, I'm so glad I got the damn port installed. The lady beside me (a lung cancer patient in her 40's) was being poked and prodded while the nurse looked for a good vein in her arm. The poor lady was in such pain. Meanwhile my port prick and IV drip were pretty painless.

I think what surprised me most was the intensity of the "meds" I got shot up with BEFORE I even got the chemo—the steroids, Benadryl, and the anti-nausea shot. They all rushed immediately to my head and made me feel super dizzy, lightheaded and slightly nauseous. Kinda like a bad drug trip or way too much booze. My dad and daughter were with me at the time and that's when I said, "Okay, I think it's time for the little two-year-old to leave the room now."

I was so foggy and sleepy that all the books and reading materials I brought with me were pretty useless. Instead, I listened to music and napped a bit.

Now—at home, six hours later—I just feel kinda out of it. Physically, I feel fine. No nausea or upset stomach or headache. But my head is still foggy. Writing this blog feels weird. It's hard to formulate coherent and flowing sentences that accurately portray my thoughts. But I'm trying.

Turns out I have to go back in tomorrow for more drugs because they only had two of the three that I was supposed to take. So number three (the ever-important Herceptin) will be administered tomorrow. Such is life.

I also found out that going forward, I'll be doing chemo every single week for the next six months or so. *Oh lord!*

But I'm still feeling strong, determined and positive. And it's so much easier to feel this way with all the amazing support I have. Hubby came home with a beautiful bouquet of roses and an empowering card that made me feel loved and cared for. Then I opened the mail and found a handwritten letter from one of my oldest friends. Yes, I said handwritten—on real stationary, with a pen. Pages and pages long with more loving words and support. I was so touched. There was also a card and beautiful picture frame filled with happy memories from one of my darling aunties in the mail. Plus, all the supportive blog, text and phone messages I received from everyone over the last 24 hours.

I swear I have the biggest support group imaginable!

So thanks to all of you for helping me get through this. You keep me strong and positive. You help me stay centered. You give me a reason to keep going. Your love fills my heart. You are amazing—each and every one of you.

CHAPTER 6

THE SAGA CONTINUES

JANUARY 4, 2012

A nother day, another dose of chemo.

Today's medicine—Herceptin—was a breeze compared to yesterday. I guess because Herceptin is actually a hormonal drug, targeted specifically at my HER2 cells and not really a traditional chemotherapy treatment. So no steroids, no Benadryl (thank god), and I was in and out in 90 minutes.

When I got home I put together my new meditation table/altar with dad (aka "grandpa") and my little munchkin, Miss M (who is great with a wrench by the way), and then I whipped up some homemade quiches that are now cooking in the oven. Take that cancer!

I also started the process of arranging childcare for Miss M. I realize I won't always have someone here as my back-up helper to watch her while I go to medical appointments. In fact, just today when we were scheduling next week's chemo treatment, I realized I couldn't schedule anything for Tuesday or Wednesday because no one would be around to watch her.

In other treatment news—the hospital where I had my MRI this past Monday called to say they want me to come in and have more scans done. It seems the MRI they did doesn't quite match up with the PET scan they did a few weeks ago, so they want to do a more detailed MRI of my leg. This is all to figure out if the cancer has spread to my bones.

Just when you think you're done with all the scans... Nope, a few more please.

I also found out my current chemo regime will continue every week for the next twelve weeks. Then I'll continue with the Herceptin weekly after that along with a few other possible chemo drugs. And I think the general plan is to just keep doing some sort of treatment like this month-after-month, year-after-year, monitoring things as we go and choosing the drugs that work best to keep the cancer at bay.

Time to go rest.

CHAPTER 7

PARENTING MY WAY THROUGH TREATMENT

JANUARY 5, 2012

Today I feel something. The chemo is definitely settling in. The effects are subtle, but there. I'm a little dizzy, light-headed, nauseous, slightly off-balance and my skin feels more sensitive and dry. I'm definitely tired—nothing major—just enough that I feel different but still able to function. While it's tough being at home with little Miss M all day, I'd much rather be at home with her than going through this while working outside the home.

Today was a big day for Miss M. She successfully completed her first day of preschool without me. She cried. I was nervous. But in the end, it was all good. I really hope her days at preschool are a fun, positive distraction from the drama of the cancer diagnosis. I worry about her a lot. I feel she's already been through so much in her short two years and can hardly believe she has to deal with this now too. Yet, despite it all she's always upbeat and full of energy. Having her around keeps us all positive and appreciating the little moments in life. Thank god for Miss M.

I still struggle with how much to tell her. While I realize she's only two-years-old, I also know she's a smart cookie and super intuitive. She realizes (or assumes) what is going on a lot of the time without us saying anything. What is scarier for her? The truth or what she makes up in her head?

I just don't want to screw her up too much. I want her to be happy and have a "normal" childhood like other kids, not forever being saddled with one tragedy after another. I want her to always have people who will play with her, take her to the playground, serve her healthy meals, smother her with hugs and kisses and adore her. I want to do my best to make up for the constant disruptions in her life and not let the cancer stop me from being the best parent I can be.

It's tough going through cancer with young kids. While you're trying to take care of yourself, you're still being depended on by someone else. You have to very carefully balance the needs of yourself and the needs of your child when you don't have very much energy to spare from the get-go. Parenting ain't easy, that's for sure.

Tomorrow, another big day. Aren't they all "big days" now? I go in for more MRI's. I'm nervous about the final results. Has the cancer spread to my bones?

We'll see...

CHAPTER 8

BLAH-DAY-BLAH

I am tired.

Physically tired, mentally tired, tired of being poked and prodded, tired of endless doctors' appointments, tired of never ending scans and tests. In the last month and a half I've had a mammogram, ultrasound, biopsy, CT scan, bone scan, PET scan, three MRIs, and an EKG. And I may still have to do a bone biopsy.

I miss my old energetic self. I miss feeling healthy. I miss being able to take care of the house, my daughter, our lives.

I hate yawning all day and feeling "spent." I hate all the little twinges of pain I feel—in my breast, arm, back and shoulder. One moment there, the next moment gone but still forcing me to stop what I'm doing. I hate that all the little tasks of my everyday life—groceries, Miss M's bath, cooking meals—have now become major energy zappers.

This is only the beginning of my journey and I can't help but think about all the months and years ahead of me. Will I ever feel like my old healthy self again?

Bitch. Bitch. Bitch. Sometimes it's just hard to stay positive.

Tomorrow's another day.

CHAPTER 9

LOVE IS THE ANSWER

JANUARY 7, 2012

Today was a better day.

Realizing it was a better day, I of course then try to figure out what helped to make it a better day. Was it because I exercised today? Because I drank my allotted one cup of coffee at 2:00 pm instead of 9:00 am? Or maybe because I ended up skipping my anti-nausea meds? Who the heck knows.

I did go for my first therapy session today. Maybe that helped, too? Not sure exactly how I feel about my therapist. But I'm willing to give her a chance.

We briefly touched on the numerous tragedies of the last three years—with so much to process and work through, it's tough to know where to begin. We set up another session for next week and agreed to meet weekly for now. I'm really hoping this will help me release any of the trauma that may still be stuck in the cells of my body. I know stress and trauma create a breeding ground for cancer. I'm also happy that hubby met with a social worker last week and has agreed to start going to therapy as well.

Having been in the caretaker position before I know how taxing it is taking care of a sick loved one. I don't want hubby to get sick too. I need him to be healthy and strong—for all of us.

I feel so much gratitude to have the husband I do. Sure, hubby has his flaws (don't we all?), but in almost nine years of marriage he has proven himself over and over. When the chips are down and life throws us a curve ball, he stays strong and supports me. When I needed to move our family 3,000 miles away to care for and be with my mom after she was diagnosed with cancer, he had my back. After my melanoma surgery and breast biopsies. he's the one who carefully removed the bandages and tended to my wounds. Through 30+ hours of labor and childbirth, he was my rock. And now, when I worry about losing my hair, gaining weight or having my breasts removed, he tells me I will always be beautiful to him and none of these things will ever make him stop loving me.

So thank you my love—for being my rock, my support system, my best friend and partner in life. I know a big reason I will get through this is because of you.

CHAPTER 10

BYE BYE GRANDPA

JANUARY 11, 2012

G randpa is gone. He left bright and early yesterday morning.

Today, Miss M is a complete and utter mess. When I ask her why she's so fussy and sad she says, "Because I miss grandpa!" Poor thing. After spending over seven whole weeks here in Ohio, it was finally time for grandpa to go home. And boy, do we miss him. It must have been divine intervention—with some help from my mom—that landed grandpa on our doorstep the night before I was scheduled to go in for my mammogram way back in November. Having him here for my initial diagnosis and being able to share the news with him firsthand, in person, was how it was meant to be. And having him here to play with Miss M and lavish her with attention and play her songs on the guitar while mommy (aka, Mamãe) went to endless doctor's appointments couldn't have been more perfect. Miss M ADORES her grandpa beyond imagination.

I can't even begin to comprehend what my dad is going through right now. Just a year and a half ago he lost his wife of 35 years to cancer and now his daughter is diagnosed with Stage 4 cancer too? That's definitely another "WTF" moment.

On our drive to the airport yesterday, he admitted that he has yet to truly process the news. Being in our home, caught up in the day-to-day madness of our lives and the holidays and the demands of Miss M didn't allow him the chance to really sit with what is going on and feel whatever he has to feel. So going home is good for him. It'll give him the chance to process it without worrying about how his tears may affect Miss M or me.

And now, the family gets ready for more visitors...

Tonight, my BFF (and Miss M's god/earth mother) Auntie Cole arrives. Yay! It'll be nice to have some more female energy in the house. And it's always nice to have your best friend around.

Tomorrow morning, I go back to the doctor for my second round of chemo. I've been trying to get everything in order these last few days while I'm feeling full of energy—just in case I feel like crap after chemo.

Yesterday, Miss M and I actually had a fabulous day together—full of smiles, love and happy moments. It was my first day alone with her in ages. We went to a children's museum, made a delicious fish dinner and had an impromptu dance party in the kitchen when LL Cool J's *Round the Way Girl* came on the radio. No tantrums. No tears. Just good times.

I realize that my goal for life now is to have as many good times as possible—to surround myself with everything and everyone that brings me joy and to let go of the stuff that brings me down. Here's to enjoying the moment and creating memories!

CHAPTER 11

TRUST YOUR INSTINCTS

JANUARY 12, 2012

Second chemo session today—so far, so good.

Auntie Cole escorted me to my chemo session today and had the honor of being the first person to meet my oncologist (who she was duly impressed and enamored with). It felt good to have my own opinion of him and intuition validated.

It was also nice to have my BFF there to hear the news about my recent MRI results.

It seems the PET scan and MRI both show that the suspicious areas in the bone marrow of my left femur are most likely cancerous. My oncologist says he's pretty certain about the results but if I need to know 110% that it's cancer, we can always do a bone biopsy. Personally, I'm not keen on going through one of those right about now so I'm going with his vibe that it's unnecessary.

Honestly, I'm not too surprised about the results. In my heart and gut I've felt from the start that my cancer had already spread to quite a few areas of my body and they always say intuition is bang on.

I continue to draw on the strength and support of those close to me and all those holding me in their thoughts and prayers. Together, we can make miracles happen. I feel it.

CHAPTER 12

WORKING IT

JANUARY 16, 2012

Yesterday evening, the auntie brigade began…

Auntie L arrived from Massachusetts and all of us couldn't be happier. Miss M was overjoyed to have Auntie L take her to "singing & dancing" class at the Y this morning. Having both Auntie Cole and Auntie L here at the same time is pure gold!

The addition of Auntie L to the household also shifted us into action mode— "to do" lists are being written, resources consulted and plans made. In true social work fashion, Auntie L—in her first day here—had me online completing my application for disability benefits (it seems Stage 4 breast cancer patients automatically qualify), and the energy seemed to carry on to Auntie Cole who took it upon herself to reorganize my pots and pans and de-clutter my kitchen counters.

Hubby and I also attended our first Tai Chi class today at Harmony Farm. The farm is magical and offers a bunch of amazing holistic services aimed at increasing balance and wellness.

Sometimes, it's hard for me to believe that I really do have cancer.

I don't feel sick. I've gone through two rounds of weekly chemo without getting nauseous, throwing up or feeling much pain at all.

I'm not really feeling any side effects. My hair is still in place. I still have energy.

Everything seems incongruent. *How can I, this seemingly healthy, normal feeling, energetic person, have Stage 4 breast cancer? Could I really have cancer spreading all through my body and bones like the scans say? Maybe they got my scans mixed up with someone else?*

I'm truly convinced that all the efforts I'm making at wellness and the support I'm receiving is what's allowing me to handle this weekly chemo with grace. I feel productive, active, more balanced, fully loved and supported. I'm sticking to my exercise routine, committed to eating healthy, continuing to meditate and I'm adding as many other wellness activities into the mix as possible (support groups, therapy, Tai Chi, visualization, yoga, Reiki).

In the back of my mind, I'm still preparing for the worst. I'm aware that all the side effects of my illness and treatment may come around to whack me in the weeks to come.

Or maybe I'll just keep cruising through this.

Regardless, I'm just enjoying the fact that, today, I feel good. Cuz in reality, today is all we got.

CHAPTER 13

TAKE THE GOOD WITH THE BAD

JANUARY 18, 2012

Week 3 chemo treatment done—and I'm still feeling pretty damn good.

Each time though, my first chemo drug seems to really hit me in a weird and intense way. My body is definitely not vibing with it. Last week I swear I could feel the Taxol flowing and burning through to the tips of my fingers and toes. This week it felt like it was burning up my chest to my face, trying to get out of my body somehow. So now there's discussion about switching to a different chemo drug in the same family (Taxotere).

Otherwise, my body seems to be tolerating all the meds pretty well. Plus, the new bone strengthening med I'm taking (Zometa) seemed to go in today without a hitch.

Yesterday, I have to admit, I was feeling some sharp stabbing pains in my breast and chest area—not so pleasant but not the worst pain I've ever felt (hello C-section and broken collarbone!). Apparently this is a common side effect of the chemo and an indication that battles are being waged in my body. The pains came. They went. I rested. And today, it's all-better.

I've said it before and I'll say it again, I truly believe the only way I'm making it through all this is because of the insane outpouring of support I'm receiving—on all levels. I've had over 5,000 visits to my blog, endless emails, hand written notes and cards, gifts/donations, text messages and offers to help with Miss M from the local community—where we've lived for only six months.

I'm especially blown away by the number of people willing to get on a plane and come out to the middle of nowhere Ohio to be with me. As my oncologist said to me the other day, "You're a real popular lady!" It is truly amazing. Having my favorite people next to me while I fight this battle makes all the difference.

So thanks again everyone. I can't even begin to express the level of gratitude and appreciation I feel.

CHAPTER 14

CREATING MEMORIES

JANUARY 22, 2012

Since posting my last blog entry, I've experienced both joy and pain—in equal measures.

Immediately after posting my last blog I crawled into bed and was overcome with a severe case of the "chills." Even with two sweaters, a bathrobe, towels and multiple blankets covering me-head-to-toe, I could not stop shivering. My bones were aching. My body was incessantly shaking. I was cold to my core. As hubby tried to do everything possible to warm me up, Auntie L Googled my symptoms and found out that this was a common reaction to the bone strengthener. *Oh lord!*

That damn Zometa—I figured it would be the easiest to tolerate seeing as it's just a "bone strengthener." For two days I was exhausted, run down, overcome with random bouts of the chills and suffering from some pretty serious pain in the core of my bones.

Despite it all, the crew and I forged ahead and continued to create glorious memories including an amazing girls' retreat at Harmony Farm. We indulged in various Reiki and massage treatments and then orchestrated a culinary extravaganza for Auntie Cole's last supper in Ohio.

To top it off, today, hubby and I actually went on a much-needed date—the classic dinner and a movie. What a gift. With hubby always working and me caught up with appointments and visitors and Miss M, the two of us hardly ever get the chance to talk or hang out any more. This really helped us reconnect.

Of course, the weekend wasn't all happy moments.

With every new visitor that arrives, the day must come for them to leave. On Saturday morning it was time for Auntie Cole to leave. Even though we all drove her to the airport and saw her off, it wasn't until the following day that Miss M registered she was no longer there. And she wasn't happy about it. Auntie Cole's energy and love is larger than life. The house feels a whole lot emptier and quieter without her in it.

Now it's Sunday night. Another week is upon us—another opportunity to continue creating glorious memories.

Make sure to make each moment a memorable one.

CHAPTER 15

EMBRACE CHANGE

JANUARY 24, 2012

J ust finished watching Obama's State of the Union address and I'm feeling inspired. Damn, that guy is a good speaker!

I'm reminded not to give up hope. Even though we sometimes have to bend and flow with life and make adjustments, we don't have to give up or compromise who we are.

This cancer is definitely forcing me to make some serious adjustments.

Even though cancer has now become my new full-time job, I won't let it to stop me from being me or pursuing my dreams. I WILL continue my career as a social worker, travel the world and be the best possible person I can be.

Cancer doesn't stand a chance. And I say all this after experiencing a day chock full of unexpected moments.

Today was supposed to be "chemo day." But when they tested me at the doctor's office, my white blood cells were too low to administer the chemo. It's funny how you're never happy about doing chemo, then when you're told you can't do it, you're suddenly sad. Of course, feeling as strong and "normal" as I do, I never imagined my blood counts would ever be anything but where they needed to be. I never anticipated my counts could be low enough to delay treatment.

I did manage to get my Herceptin today though. All is not lost.

And now I'm taking another medication—Leukine. It's a shot that's supposed to increase white blood counts by going into the bone marrow and encouraging the growth of good cells. *Will it ever end?* Possible side effects? Bone pain. Chills. Flu symptoms. *Damn! Not again.* My oncologist says this may become a regular part of my regime as I go through treatment. *Fun! Fun!*

The new plan is to take the Leukine shots for three days then wait and see if my counts go up. If they're close to 2,000 on Monday, I should be good to go for chemo on Tuesday.

What Auntie L and I have taken from the latest change in plans is—that life is unpredictable. As my mom always used to say, "The only constant in life is change." So you'd better learn to adapt.

And I am—Adapting. Accepting. Living. Growing.

Tomorrow is another day. Anything is possible.

CHAPTER 16

FIGURE OUT WHAT'S IMPORTANT

JANUARY 28, 2012

W hen you're faced with your own mortality it causes you to reevaluate what's important.

At the ripe old age of 37, death is not something I really contemplated before now. And then, wham—you're diagnosed with Stage 4 cancer and your whole perspective changes.

I know some people facing serious illness and terminal disease may be tempted to continue living their lives just as they had before—changing nothing. Although I continue with the day-to-day tasks of everyday living, I've also been overcome by this strong desire to prioritize—to decide what's truly deserving of my time.

I don't want to waste my time on bullshit.

I think questioning what's truly important is a good exercise for everyone to do. *Are you spending the time you have in a nourishing and fulfilling way? Do you enjoy your work? Do you enjoy your time outside of work? Do you make decisions in line with what you truly want out of life?*

Immediately following my diagnosis these questions started to creep into my head.

So what sorts of things are important to me? Family and friends.

Having this ongoing rotation of all my favorite people coming out to Ohio to help us is such a gift. Just this morning Auntie L finally headed home. *Sniff! Sniff!* Miss M is still in a state of denial asking, "Where's Auntie L? I wanna play!" Thank god the family and friend brigade continues tomorrow with Auntie M. Having all these loved ones around is not only helping me, it's helping Miss M big time in terms of dealing with all of the changes cancer has thrust onto our family.

So what else is important? Spending time doing things that bring me joy—dancing, traveling the world, being in nature, watching sunsets, listening to music, getting engrossed in a really good book, learning new things, helping others, being in NYC, meeting new people...

But even though I've figured out what's important to me, the hardest step is incorporating these things into my life—making them a priority.

So let's all do it together. Let's make the effort to prioritize the things that bring us joy. Find a few moments each day to do something enriching and enjoyable—something that makes your day a bit better and makes this life worth living.

If not now—when?

CHAPTER 17

GREEN LIGHT

JANUARY 30, 2012

I got the green light today to go ahead with chemo again. My white blood cell count needed to be around 2,000 and it was 2,500. Understandably, I've now become slightly obsessed with raising my white blood count.

Tomorrow is round four of chemo. Even after a month of this I still get nervous every week. What I'm nervous about is not entirely clear. *Maybe I'm afraid of something going wrong? Afraid of a bad reaction? Feeling pain? Afraid of the unknown?* I don't know. Life is just really one unknown after another. I guess that's why so many of us spend so much time in fear.

The best thing I can do is try to process and understand what I'm feeling (hello therapy!) and then just come back to the present moment. Root myself in the here and now, the task at hand and not get caught up in the stinkin' thinking about the if's, but's, and could's of life.

In other news—my hair is officially falling out. Not sure how long it'll take before it's too thin for me to justify keeping it. Pondering on getting a super cute blond pixie wig. It's the style I've always wanted to get but never had the balls to commit to. I also feel it's necessary to pay homage to my hair—to say thank you for being one of my favorite features. Thanks for helping me define my style. Thanks for keeping my ears warm in the winter months. I will miss you.

Round four of the family and friends brigade has arrived—Auntie M—and she is spoiling Miss M rotten! Of course Miss M loves every moment of it. It's so amazing to have this much love around to buoy us and keep us afloat. Making sure Miss M gets through all this relatively unscathed is so important to me and I cannot do it alone.

Big shout-outs and thanks to my amazing family and friends brigade! And to all the other beautiful people out there supporting me in this journey. The things you do are not going unnoticed.

CHAPTER 18

MY NEW JOB

FEBRUARY 1, 2012

Yesterday's chemo session was one of the smoothest thus far. There were no extreme reactions, it was faster than usual and I had minimal chemo fogginess at the end of the day.

We did switch from Taxol to Taxotere which was much better. Next week we're switching from IV Benadryl to regular over-the-counter Benadryl—at a lower dosage (so I should be even less foggy at the end of the day).

I'm starting to realize what a full-time job it is to manage a serious chronic illness and strive to be a truly healthy human being—endless doctor's appointments; blood work; treatment consultations with genetics counselors, physical therapists and specialists; medical bills; psychotherapy; support groups; finding time for physical exercise, meditation and complementary treatments; researching every option, alternative, supplement and suggestion; eating the right things and not eating the things I really want to eat...

My lord!

When I dropped off Miss M at daycare this week to go to chemo she grabbed me and whined, "No, I don't want you to go the doctor's."

When she was playing with hubby the other day she said, "I can't right now, I have to get blood work." What other two-year-old says this stuff? As much as we try to shield her from what's going on, it still seeps through. How can it not? Especially when I literally am going to the doctor five days a week.

Taking care of myself is my new full-time job. And although I'm not getting paid in the traditional sense of the word, I guess you could say the payment I receive is the continuation of my life.

CHAPTER 19

ROUGH WATERS

FEBRUARY 2, 2012

The last 24 hours have been pretty rough.

Last night I woke up at 3:00 am overcome with chills and shaking uncontrollably. I begged hubby to layer me with blankets, towels, bathrobes—anything to warm me up. I ended up with a slight fever, an unrelenting headache that took almost seven hours to get rid of, random spells of nausea and discomfort in the freakin' follicles of my hair (which I hear is common when you start losing your hair).

So now we've decided to hold off on more Leukine shots (the suspected culprit in most of my side effects). Then we'll see how my blood counts are on Monday—meaning I may, or may not be able to continue with chemo next week.

There's talk of using an alternative to the Leukine and spreading out chemo to once every three weeks. Who knows? Right now, all I can do is get through the next 24 hours.

I do know that I'm gathering every possible immune boosting remedy I can find to tackle my white blood count naturally. Fingers crossed it'll help.

Right now, I must sleep. They all can't be good days, eh?

CHAPTER 20

TRUSTING THE PATH

FEBRUARY 4, 2012

F ear not, I am feeling better.

In the days since my not-so-fun reaction to the Leukine, I have rallied back to life and gone on to create some beautiful memories.

Yesterday was yet another journey into nearby Yellow Springs with Miss M and Auntie M. Then today, after dropping off Auntie M at the airport, hubby, Miss M and I went on a family adventure that included a trip to the circus! It was especially cool because not only was it Miss M's first time at the circus, it was also mine. Both she and I were totally transfixed. What fun!

During intermission as hubby and Miss M went down to look at the elephants, I relaxed in my seat and started thinking. *How is it going to be to live my life with a bald head? Going to the circus? The library? Grocery shopping? All with this bold proclamation of my current health status?* It's almost like wearing a big colorful name tag that says, "Hi, I'm Terri. I have cancer."

The deal with my hair that sparked all these thoughts is that millions of hairs are falling out basically every time I touch my head. Luckily I had a thick mop of hair to begin with, so this thinning out process is taking a while. But it's almost becoming more hassle than it's worth to keep the little that's left. I feel myself inching closer and closer to saying, "Fuck it!" and just shaving it off.

I've always believed that everything happens for a reason—Miss M coming into our lives at the perfect time to distract us from the turmoil of the last three years and keep us smiling; my mom being sick at a time in my life when I could pack everything up and move across the country to take care of her; her sickness affording me the opportunity to stay at home and raise Miss M; hubby getting a job in Ohio where living on one salary is possible and living with cancer is easier in so many ways; us being essentially homeless for six months before moving to Ohio so that I could appreciate just having a roof over our heads and not get caught up in negativity about living in a small town and leaving my beloved NYC.

I trust that somewhere there is a reason for my breast cancer diagnosis as well.

I'll let you know once I figure it out.

CHAPTER 21

NEW BEGINNINGS

FEBRUARY 6, 2012

Wow! What a day!

I finally did it—chopped off my hair (or what was left of it). Hubby hooked me up and gave me a fashionable buzz cut with a fade. I think I kinda look like Hillary Swank in *Boys Don't Cry*. Miss M watched the whole thing, eventually joining in our "hair cutting party" by getting a trim herself.

It's funny how the anticipation of an event is always scarier than the event itself. And when you're all done, you realize it really wasn't that big a deal after all.

So there we go—big crazy, scary, life hurdle done. Check.

The other amazing news is that I met with my oncologist today to have my white blood cell count tested and it's off the charts! It went from 2,500 last Monday to 9,600 this Monday. Craziness! I walked out of his office crying big ol' tears of joy.

My doctor of course is a bit perplexed at how this happened. I assured him it had to be because of all the supplements, meditations and guided imagery I was doing. He smiled at me in that, "Okay, whatever you say," kinda way.

Thank you to all who offered suggestions on how to boost my white blood count. It worked. All of this means no more Leukine shots. Yay, one less pharmaceutical I have to put in my body.

So what am I doing to keep my white blood count boosted? Taking a crapload of supplements and vitamins. Plus I'm drinking lots of green tea and special therapeutic mushroom tea, trying to squeeze in 30-45 minutes of exercise most days of the week and sticking to my uber healthy eating plan.

The other thing I think has been really helping is my guided imagery and meditations. I've been visualizing my white blood count multiplying and spreading to every inch of my body during daily meditation sessions. If visualization can help basketball players get more free throw shots, why can't it help me get more white blood cells?

I just finished reading an amazing little book, "The Power of the Mind to Heal," that reinforced my deep-seated belief that our brains, thoughts, visions and mindset greatly influence our health and ability to heal.

So with that, I celebrate the beauty of today and head into tomorrow's chemo session with confidence.

There is hope. There is always hope.

CHAPTER 22

FORGING ON

FEBRUARY 9, 2012

It's never a good idea to tempt fate. Everyone around me got a cold and I, on more than one occasion, commented, "Oh, how interesting that everyone but the cancer patient has a cold!" Then of course three days later, I too got the cold. You wanna get cocky? Take that.

Interesting how magnified everything becomes when you have cancer. Suddenly, that little harmless cold is a menacing force dictating important decisions about your life.

But despite the menacing cold, I continue to forge on—new therapist, check; seminar on the benefits of acupuncture and Chinese medicine, check; figure out how to tie a head scarf, check.

All week my darling Auntie D has been here with the family. It's so interesting having my aunties come back-to-back, one after another, and seeing the different energies each of them brings—proactive and indulgent Auntie L, nature loving and matter-of-fact Auntie M and now laid back and youthful Auntie D (who was the perfect person to have around for the monumental "hair cutting party"). Their visits have helped me (and Miss M and hubby) on so many levels and we've created so many moments of joy together. I really do come from an amazing lineage of strong, compassionate women.

What a gift.

Auntie D leaves tomorrow. After that, hubby and I are on our own for one whole week. *Oh lord!* Maybe this is a good thing? It'll be the first week we've been without a houseguest since this whole thing started back in November. I think we can handle it. We'll just have to call on our local resources here in Ohio.

Chemo went by without a hitch this week. Hopefully next week will be the same.

CHAPTER 23

THE CIRCLE OF SUPPORT

FEBRUARY 11, 2012

I t's been an interesting couple of days.

Yesterday I woke up feeling like crap. I was feeling sorry for myself and got into a bad case of the "fuck its"—as in—*Fuck it!* I'm just gonna eat almost a whole bag of Stacy's cinnamon and sugar pita chips—*Fuck it!* I might as well throw in a couple of chocolate chip cookies too—*And fuck it!* I'm not gonna exercise today. I'm too sick... *Waahhh! Waahhh!*

By the time hubby got home I was a mess. He told me to get my ass up to bed and go to sleep. Of course, even a simple command such as this is not easy for me. Remember that amazing lineage of strong and compassionate women I come from? Well, they are also notorious "doers" who take care of everyone else and have difficulty taking care of themselves.

But last night I remembered what my new therapist said to me. "Doing nothing is doing something. It's taking care of yourself. Doing nothing helps you heal."

So I did it. I went to bed at 6:00 pm and slept all the way till this morning. Today, I'm feeling much, much better.

I've also been getting lots of concerned calls, texts and emails about how hubby and I are going to handle things on our own next week. I think I need to chat for a moment about how amazing the folks in Ohio are. From the displays of generosity and spirit I've seen here, I know in my heart that all we have to do is ask and what we need will be taken care of.

Just today Miss M and I went for lunch at our favorite spot, Bakehouse, and the owner personally came out to say hi to us. Turns out she's been reading my blog. She refused to take my money and promised to keep me in her prayers. I'm guessing she found out about my story from my dear friend Amy who organized the delicious gift of weekly bread deliveries. *Thanks Amy!* And these are just a few examples of the outpouring of support and love coming my way.

The parents and staff at Miss M's preschool, Overfield, have also gone out of their way to offer support. They've made me a gorgeous prayer shawl, bought me organic medicinal mushroom soup from Dayton and offer to help with Miss M whenever and however I need it.

But it's not just the folks here in Ohio who have been going the extra mile. Tickets are already close to selling-out for a benefit concert back east organized by a close circle of friends and family who call themselves the Graceful Woman Warrior committee. All proceeds will go straight to me and my family to help pay for treatment, medical bills, travel costs, childcare and everything else you need to kick some cancer ass.

I've also got strangers sending me supplements to build my immune system and others offering to send me scarves to wear on my newly-shaven head. Not to mention the gazilions who have donated money. Can I tell you how heavenly it is to have money set aside in a separate account just to pay the medical bills that keep coming in? Really. It's hard for me to wrap my brain around this much love and support.

Then I think of my mom and remember when she was battling Stage 4 cancer how thousands and thousands of people from all over the world came out of the woodwork with a story to tell about how my mom had touched their lives—listened to their story, offered a few wise words, gave them a hug or just a smile and her attention. I'm not sure she even realized what an impact she had on other people's lives. I hope she does now.

I guess I am my mother's daughter.

May she offer a lesson to all of us. To put our best foot forward. To be present. To make connections. You never know how your actions may affect the life of another person.

CHAPTER 24

TRY-AND-TRY-AGAIN

FEBRUARY 14, 2012

Today I went in for my weekly blood check and the damn cold terrorized my white blood counts. Last week I was at 9,600. This week I'm down to 1,400. I need to be around 2,000 to do chemo.

But I did get my Herceptin (and a bonus afternoon to myself while Miss M was in daycare). This also means I won't have to deal with any yucky side effects while no one is here to provide back-up support.

Maybe it was meant to be this way after all?

I also attended my first breast cancer support group at the local hospital. Interestingly enough, the topic of discussion was alternative and complementary treatments—right up my alley.

I spoke of how I'm trying to keep my white blood cells up by using natural methods instead of pharmaceuticals. Everyone seemed very intrigued at this foreign and unfamiliar way of doing things. Turns out that only me and one other lady have ever tried anything other than what the doctors tell you to do. While a lot of the holistic stuff just seems second nature to me, I'm realizing a big segment of the population has no clue about this sort of stuff. We went on to have a lively discussion about energy work, supplements, the power of the mind and then we traded stories about losing our hair and having fun with wigs. All in all, it was a great night.

One thing I continuously notice in my journey is how much younger I am than all the other cancer patients I encounter. I would so love to chat with other cancer moms who are trying to balance their needs with those of their family—trying to figure out who's gonna watch the kids while they go for their umpteenth MRI or how to be fully present and available as a mom, even when you're totally shot from chemo.

I've put calls into two organizations to find a "young mentor" and signed up for another cancer support group that is specifically for young folks. We'll see.

In the meantime, I continue to gather wisdom from every source possible. You never know where the answers will lie.

CHAPTER 25

TAP INTO YOUR ABUNDANCE

FEBRUARY 17, 2012

Wow, what an intense couple of days!

First, I have to admit it's been a bit of an adjustment flying solo this week. Taking care of myself, the day-to-day household stuff and a two-year-old is totally exhausting. It doesn't help matters that Miss M has been cranky as all hell this week—tantrums for every single little thing. I mean everything.

Then, a miracle—today Miss M and I had a beautiful day together. No tantrums, just quality time at the park listening to the birds sing and playing on the see-saw. We had a nice lunch at Bakehouse and a giddy kitchen dance party with old school tracks like De La Soul's *Me, Myself, and I.* Classic! Miss M and I were striking poses, doing yoga moves and laughing it up.

But wait, there's more...

My girlfriend Liz in NYC sent me the most delicious healthy chocolate I have ever tasted and folks keep sending me these amazing books. Thank you to whoever it was that sent the book, "Between Me and the River: Living Beyond Cancer: A Memoir," and to the stranger from Bowen who sent me the blessing, "For a Friend, On the Arrival of

Illness," written by John O'Donohue. Thanks to the fabulous staff at Miss M's preschool who sent a touching card and informed me that Miss M's tuition for the remainder of the school year would be taken care of. Hello! This card actually generated tears—not a common occurrence with me. Then my west coast friend, Lisa Marie, took an hour out of her busy schedule to give me a free nutrition session and cleared up a number of questions I had about my diet.

And just when you think the outpouring of love couldn't get any bigger, it does.

After my dad posted about my situation on his site, spiderrobinson.com and boingboing.net, the science fiction community and über intellectuals came out to support my cause big time.

To top it off, I heard from my good friends on Bowen Island that they want to plan a benefit for me! Another benefit? For me? This community of around 3,000 people who just two years ago rallied to help my mom during her battle with cancer still have enough energy and love to take up the rally once again?

This has all gone way beyond what I imagined. It reminded me of the importance of believing in abundance. It does exist. There is enough love for everyone. If you are open to it and ready to embrace it, the love is always there.

This is my new challenge, the challenge for all of us—to acknowledge and receive love and abundance and then put it back out there into the world.

Deep gratitude to each and every one of you.

CHAPTER 26

MEETING LIFE'S CHALLENGES

FEBRUARY 22, 2012

I was able to have my chemo again this week—my white blood count was at 4,500 (not the supreme ideal of 9,600 that it was a few weeks ago, but good enough). It was a long-ass day and I ended up being there pretty much the whole day. Of course it was the one time I didn't pack a lunch so I subsisted on fruit, almonds and some free peanut butter crackers (that were not on my approved diet list, but at that point I really didn't care).

I also had my monthly Zometa medication (the one that left me shivering and shaking uncontrollably for hours on end last month). We were expecting a repeat performance last night. Thankfully it did not appear. I've heard from other breast cancer warriors that the same thing happened to them—the first time was the hardest and then it subsequently got much easier.

Today, I am weak. I am tired. But feeling okay.

I'm noticing the toughest thing for me to do is be a good parent to Miss M.

Everything else—no problem. Dinner, I got that. Dishes, I can handle. Exercise, I can still do it. But dealing with Miss M and all her toddler tantrums and defiance—god that takes a lot of energy—to enforce the rules, be consistent, come up with creative ways to get her to do what I want her to do, to beat her at her own game. You have to be so on the ball and I am just not these days.

I am super thankful for my visitors (many of whom are also moms) that give me tips and show me new ways of parenting. I am thankful for their energy when I have none, for their ideas when my chemo brain robs me of my own and for their guidance because my own mother is no longer here to offer it.

This week my childhood friend Auntie A is here with her three-year-old daughter. It's beautiful having them here. Auntie A is an amazing parent—full of energy and totally devoted to being a great mom. She's wonderful with Miss M and I'm learning a lot from her.

After a week without "in home" help, I'm thoroughly grateful to have someone here who can help me get everything done—all while exchanging parenting woes and catching up on the mysteries of life.

I know that I need to get myself some permanent help around the house but it's so difficult. I feel like I'm losing my ability to be a really good parent. And I don't know what to do about it. It hurts me to think that I have to hire someone to do the number one most important thing to me—parenting my daughter. I hate the cancer for that—for robbing me of my ability to be the kick-ass mom I used to be.

Throughout all the turmoil of the last few years—my mom's passing, the endless moves, new people, new situations—I have been Miss M's only constant. Her rock. And now I'm coming apart at the seams. *How does this not impact her? How do you process all these major life changes with a toddler?*

Aaahhhh, life's challenges. They're never ending. And the answers are not always immediately visible or available. I guess the key is to not give up—to keep searching, keep pushing forward and then just hope for the best.

CHAPTER 27

CHOOSE WELL

FEBRUARY 25, 2012

First of all, big thanks go out to everyone who offered parenting advice and reassurance after my last blog entry. I've taken a lot of what was said to heart and I'm applying the wisdom I'm gaining. Things are getting a bit easier.

Today was actually a beautiful day. Miss M was in a great mood. Hubby and I got a few moments to chat and connect and of course bust some dance moves with Miss M. It was good ol' fashioned quality family time without stepping foot outside the house.

I also had a tremendous experience today. I went for another Reiki session in my quest to naturally boost my immune system. My Reiki practitioner and I immediately bonded. She too was handed a terminal diagnosis. Years later she's alive and well—thanks to her kick-ass attitude and a whole bunch of holistic treatments and Eastern medicine.

Our Reiki session was intense and healing for both of us. I was amazed at the internal shift I felt energetically when she placed her hands in different positions over my body. It was way more intense than any other Reiki session I've had before. I immediately signed up for more.

I'm still determined to explore every possible option to do this naturally.

Even when it seems life is backing you into a corner, you always have a choice. I cannot control the fact that I have cancer. But I can control how I deal with it. I can choose not to let it ruin my life. I can choose to keep on living in spite of it.

It's your life. Choose well.

CHAPTER 28

REALITY CAN BE A BITCH

FEBRUARY 27, 2012

Normally I try to remain optimistic. But in the last few days I've been Googling up metastatic breast cancer blogs to read other women's stories. To be honest, I usually try to avoid reading much of anything about metastatic breast cancer. The stories are not always good. The statistics, not so encouraging. Quite a few of the blogs come to an abrupt end—when three years or five years later the courageous women suddenly get really sick and then they're gone.

The reality is that the odds aren't in my favor.

Stage 4 metastatic breast cancer is a different beast than all other breast cancers. When you're diagnosed with Stage 1, 2, or even 3, the prognosis is pretty decent. You go through a year or so of really intense treatment, surgery, pain and drama. You get rid of the cancer and then hope it never comes back.

But metastatic breast cancer has no cure. We don't just do treatment for a year or so. We do treatment for the rest of our lives. Metastatic cancer is more like an intense chronic illness that can take your life at any moment.

Sometimes, it's hard for me to relate to the journeys of other women with earlier stage cancer. Yeah, Stage 2 cancer sucks. But you won't have to be in chemo for the rest of your life. Your cancer will likely go into remission. Your odds of survival are pretty good. You'll likely get your life back again.

It's different for me.

That being said, hubby and I can no longer feel the massive tumors that used to be in my left breast. In my appointment with my oncologist today, he confirmed that he could no longer feel the tumors either. It's insane. Something that was over 6 cm big only two months ago is now reduced to scar tissue. I know my fighting spirit, along with my commitment to both Eastern and Western medicine is working.

Of course we have to wait till April when I do my next set of scans to know the whole story. But I told Dr. K that I'm going to be his miracle patient. He just smiled, as he always does, and said something along the lines of, "I would love that."

I will never give up hope, but reality is still damn scary sometimes.

CHAPTER 29

BLAZING GLORY

MARCH 3, 2012

Last night the Graceful Woman Warrior committee went all out and orchestrated one seriously kick-ass party. How do I know? Because I got to be there—even though I was in Ohio—thanks to modern technology. Yay Skype! My own impromptu Ohio house party got to be a part of the big Massachusetts party. We heard the music, saw the dancing, chatted with the people, shared some laughs (and some red wine). It was a beautiful thing.

I have to throw out a BIG THANKS to the entire GWW committee who busted their asses to make sure the party was a success. You guys rocked it! You freely gave your time, energy, inspiration and love to create the best party ever.

If cancer is the price I have to pay, the cross I have to bear to reap the blessings of having such a gracious, thoughtful, and caring circle of family and friends, then so be it.

When you get right down to it, aren't relationships and personal connections really what make life worth living? Spending time with someone you care about, watching your children grow and learn, feeling the dizzying intensity of new love, exchanging ideas and lending a helping hand—it's all based on connection and relationships.

The number of connections I've made since being diagnosed with metastatic breast cancer a mere three months ago still blows me away.

Being my mother's daughter I naturally seek out and make connections wherever I go. I value the relationships I develop with everyone I meet. I believe that every person I encounter has something to teach me.

So thank you to my family, friends, all the people that attended the benefit last night and all those who continue to support me from afar. My gratitude cup runneth over.

At my Reiki session today my Reiki practitioner, Renee, mentioned that she just doesn't get a "sickness" vibe from me. In the past she's felt other people's illness while doing work on them and is often called on for her intuition with these things. But with me, the Stage 4 cancer energy isn't coming through. Who knows? Guess we'll see when I get my next scan.

In the meantime, I will continue to blaze my glorious trail of healing, wellness and connection. Take that cancer!

CHAPTER 30

ASK FOR IT

MARCH 13, 2012

This is the third week in a row I kept my white blood count high enough to do chemo! I think my entire medical team is a little amazed and flabbergasted—but also so genuinely happy for me and encouraging of the alternative and complementary path I am taking—which is awesome. Having a medical team that is supportive and optimistic makes all the difference. My oncology nurses are continually suggesting and finding ways to tweak my treatment to make it as non-invasive as possible and Dr. K tries to maximize my quality of life while still doing what is necessary to beat up the cancer.

This week Dr. K supported my request to hold back on the Zometa. After recently reading some horrible stories about Zometa—including ongoing lawsuits, reports of jaw problems and even bone fractures (isn't this the drug that is supposed to PREVENT fractures?)—I've been seriously thinking about scaling back or not taking it anymore. When I discussed it with Dr. K he said he'd be willing to hold off until after we get the results of my next scan. Then we can decide.

I'm really trying to understand what cancer has come to show me. *Why did it come? What lessons am I supposed to learn from this?*

I know one of the lessons cancer has come to teach me is to ask for what I want—not to use passive aggressiveness or guilt to get what I want, not to assume that people know exactly what I need and not to worry so much about hurting or pleasing other people.

I remember a scene in the movie *50/50* where the main character (who ends up getting cancer) is faced with a situation that upsets him. But he doesn't say anything. He just stuffs down his feelings not wanting to ruffle any feathers.

That scene stuck with me. I realize I do that, too. And I remember reading somewhere that cancer has a tendency to develop in folks like us—the ones who don't speak up—who try to do everything right and who can't ask for what they want or need.

So now I'm trying my best to make my voice heard—to ask for what I need and not feel bad about it. Instead of accepting that I have to take Zometa, I'm telling my doctor I really don't want to.

For anyone out there facing a medical issue, I implore you to get a good team and fight for what feels right to you. We know our bodies better than anyone else. It's up to us to speak out and be active decision makers in our own treatment plans.

Make the choice to be an active decision maker in your life each and every day.

Here's to another beautiful day and many more to come.

CHAPTER 31

KEEP ON KEEPING ON

MARCH 28, 2012

I have good news and bad news.

The bad news is that my white blood count has dropped. The good news is that I got my chemo anyway. With only one more week to go in this round of chemo, I'm just eager to get it done with. Luckily, Dr. K is on the same page.

The other beautiful thing about yesterday's appointment was that both Auntie L and hubby got to join me. Hubby finally got to meet the fabulous Dr. K and my kick-ass nurses. I had the pleasure of having two of my favorite people there with me—a nice change since I usually fly solo to all my appointments. Dr. K was kind enough to sit with us for over half an hour, patiently answering questions and discussing plans for the months ahead. He is such a kind and caring doctor. I'm so glad I went with my gut feeling and chose him.

I've agreed to suck it up and take one more shot of the Leukine to boost my white blood count. Hopefully that'll keep my counts high enough to get my last dose of chemo next week. If all goes according to plan, it'll be scans the following week, results shortly thereafter and then a break from chemoland with a fabulous trip to visit my "crew" in Toronto with Miss M. *Woohoo!*

Our visit with Dr. K yesterday reminded me how endless this process is—how I'll be forced to manage my illness and symptoms for years and years to come.

I think one of the most difficult things for me to swallow about my new life with metastatic breast cancer is the reality that I will likely be on some type of pharmaceutical drug for the rest of my life. It's a tough pill to swallow for this "all natural" girl.

So yes, I'm almost done with my first round of chemo. But even though I applaud this first step I also realize there is so much more to come. And although I feel pretty damn good these days, I may not always feel this way.

The truth is that when I allow myself to think about how devastating Stage 4 breast cancer can be, my heart beats a little faster. A sensation of terror flows through me. I get scared.

I try not to think about how bad things could be and instead focus on the success stories—like Katherine Russell Rich who has been living with metastatic breast cancer for almost 20 years. These are the people that keep me going—that keep hope alive.

I have to keep hope alive.

CHAPTER 32

HAPPY BIRTHDAY MOM

MARCH 30, 2012

Niagra Falls 2005

Today is my mom's birthday. She would have been 64.

Unfortunately, as you already know, my mom passed away almost two years ago—cancer.

Today I celebrate her birth and remember the brilliance of Jeanne Robinson—dancer, writer, choreographer, Buddhist, sister, wife, friend, aunt and of course, mother. I could go on and on about how kick-ass my mom was. Anyone who met her knows exactly what I'm talking about.

I took some time by myself today to walk in the woods and connect with her—listening to the birds, watching the ripples on the pond, feeling the breeze, telling mom how much I miss her, wishing she were here with me during my own struggle with cancer. Crying.

I've been crying all day—thinking about her, remembering, watching old videos of her and Miss M, looking at photos.

In doing so, I realize that amidst all the turmoil and sadness of mom being sick there were still so many moments of joy, laughter, dance, music and love. The videos and photos were full of them—my mom and dad singing and playing guitar while Miss M bounces up and down to the beat, the family walking through the magnificent rainforests of Bowen Island, Miss M giggling and my mom soaking up every possible piece of her and the love we all felt just being together.

I'm so glad Miss M was born when she was. Miss M helped us stay rooted in the moment and not dwell on the fact that mom was sick. She made my mom so happy, allowing her to forget about the cancer. Miss M and my mom had a special bond. Even now, Miss M continues to lighten our days during our second round of cancer. It's no coincidence that she arrived when she did.

Today, on my mom's birthday, I remember all the good memories. Today I give thanks.

Thank you, mom, for being such an inspiration. Thank you for showing me it's okay to be a parent and still go after your own dreams. Thank you for loving me unconditionally. Thank you for modeling compassion. Thank you for being my #1 cheerleader and helping me become the strong, confident and loving woman I am today. Thank you for being my mom.

Happy Birthday.

CHAPTER 33

EAST MEETS WEST

APRIL 1, 2012

I'm trying so hard to find the balance between Eastern and Western medicine. What I've noticed so far is that Western medicine hurts a lot and Eastern medicine takes a lot of time and energy. It's also so interesting to me how East and West approach the same disease in two totally different ways.

Take my recent white blood count drop as an example. The doctors and nurses were not surprised about the drop (they've actually been more surprised about the count going up lately). They assured me it was just the chemo doing what it does. When I asked if my drinking and not eating healthy the week before could have contributed to the drop, they said, "Nope."

But when I told my acupuncturist/Chinese medicine practitioner about the white blood cell drop she was surprised—especially since it had been going up steadily for the last month. The first question she asked me was, "What did you eat?"

Two totally different responses.

I know in my gut that living healthy is going to help me against the cancer—as are my Reiki sessions (for which I largely credit my ability to go on a seven-mile bike ride with Miss M this morning). My Reiki practitioner is amazing. Without me even having to tell her where it hurts, Renee instinctively knows exactly where to go. I always feel so much more balanced after our sessions. As she says, it's "massage for your soul."

The reality is that staying healthy takes a lot of time, energy and money—and a willingness to remain open to every option and possibility.

I will continue to chart my own path, to live this life as long as I possibly can and to make it a good one.

CHAPTER 34

AN ICON GONE

APRIL 4, 2012

I'm a jumble of emotions today. If I were still getting my period I'd say I was PMS-ing.

This morning I sat down to breakfast with Miss M, opened my email and came across a post from fellow metastatic breast cancer warrior, Katherine O'Brien. Then I started to cry.

This is how I learned the ever-inspirational Katherine Russell Rich died this week—on Tuesday April 3rd to be exact, my last day of chemo.

Katherine Russell Rich was a sassy, vibrant icon for those of us in the mets community. She was originally diagnosed and treated for breast cancer at age 32. Five years later, the cancer returned and spread. Despite the not-so-encouraging prognosis of Stage 4 breast cancer, Katherine surprised everyone and went on to live another 18 years— virtually unheard of in our metastatic world.

Her book, "The Red Devil: To Hell With Cancer—And Back," was one of the first I read after I was diagnosed. I just loved her sarcasm and wry sense of humor. I remember reading it while doing chemo and literally laughing out loud. It was just what I needed in that moment.

I'm actually kind of surprised by how much emotion and sadness her death kicked up in me. It's not like I knew her personally. And yet I feel connected to her somehow. I guess it's more about what she represents. She was my ideal, my icon, the person who gave me hope. She was invincible to me. As long as she was alive there was hope for me too.

Her death reminds me that none of us are invincible. Even if I live as long as she did, I still may not see Miss M get married, or get to enjoy retirement with hubby or experience the joy of being a grandparent. Her death is a reminder of the seriousness of my condition.

On the flip side, I appreciate how openly Katherine shared her journey—how she offered hope for so many of us. I admire her wisdom and the way she embraced life and how in going after her own dreams, she's inspiring me to figure out what the hell I want from this life and go for it.

The hard truth is that there are no guarantees. Everybody suffers. Life is not fair. Accepting my new reality is not easy. And yet I must do it. My motto over the last few years has been, "It is what it is." Take what comes and keep making the best out of each and every day that we are given.

Thank you, Katherine, for helping initiate me into this new club. May you be at peace. And say "hi" to my mom if you see her up there.

CHAPTER 35

SCAN DAYS

APRIL 9, 2012

I found a new blog site today and its entry into my life couldn't have come at a better time. The blog is, "Miracle Survivors—Inspiration and Information for Cancer Thrivers." The lady at its helm is Tami Boehmer. Her approach to life and cancer completely resonates with me. She has even written a book full of survival stories about people who essentially cured themselves or lived way beyond expectations, "From Incurable to Incredible."

Hope is super important to me right now as I get ready to face the results of my first set of scans. Today I had my mammogram and bone scan. Tomorrow is the PET scan. We meet with the doctor on Thursday to get the results and chat about the next step in my treatment plan.

I'm nervous. But I'm not. I'm worried. But I'm not. I know things are better than they were five months ago when I was first diagnosed. Back then, I was in pain. Now, my only pains seem to be from the drugs they give me. Back then, there were massive lumps in my breast. Now, not so much. I know overall that I'm better. I've lost 15 lbs. I have much more respect for my body. I've rekindled my regular exercise and meditation routine. I'm in therapy. I'm accepting more help and giving up on the need to be perfect—allowing myself to say no.

These are so many changes that I've been meaning to get around to doing, but never did—until I got Stage 4 cancer. I guess the Universe's earlier attempts at getting me to change (like my brush with melanoma in 2008) were not heard, so things got a bit extreme. *Okay, I hear you now. I'm working on it.*

As I go through this week, I recognize the nervous energy inside of me. It's so easy to get scared, assume the worst, worry about all the things that could go wrong. But why? Where will that get me? What will that accomplish? I know things can be bad. But why can't I believe in good? Assume the best? Trust the Universe? Seek possibilities? Even if the best possible outcome doesn't appear, at least I'll be in a better mood for the journey.

Thank you Tami Boehmer for your words—for giving me hope and reminding me that we have more power in life than we think we do.

CHAPTER 36

HELL YEAH!!

APRIL 12, 2012

The results of the scans are in and the news is good—better than good!

My mammogram, bone scan and PET scan show no more cancer in my bones or in my lymph nodes. Hell yeah!

Yes, you read that right. The cancer in my femur bone, back and a gazillion lymph nodes from my chest to my throat is no longer showing up on any of the scans. The only remaining detectable cancer in my body seems to be confined to my left breast—and even that has shrunk considerably, down from 6 cm and 4 cm to a measly .5 cm and 1.5 cm.

What? You wanna piece of me cancer? I don't think so, bitch!

I'm still in a bit of shock. I find myself randomly weeping tears of joy at odd times during the day. I'm trying to fully digest what this means.

In the here and now, this means I get a nice chemo vacation—another hell yeah! I'll continue on weekly Herceptin, plus I'm adding a new pill—Tamoxifen—to the mix. I must admit I'm not thrilled about taking the Tamoxifen, but I'm gonna give it a chance.

I'll continue to meet with my oncologist on a regular basis and monitor my body for any suspicious changes. Then I go for another set of scans in about four months.

And what do I do with this gift of time? Travel of course!

I'm off to Toronto Saturday followed by visits to my family and friends in NYC (a given), Massachusetts, Nashville and Bowen Island. I'm cramming it all in before my next set of scans. I've got to do it now while I'm feeling good. I have no guarantee this gift I've been given—of time, health and life—will continue, so I must seize the day.

It's weird. Even though the news is beyond good, it almost feels too good to be true.

I know I must continue to use this cancer as a teaching tool—to see that it has come to awaken something inside me, to keep me in check, to be a lifelong partner that forces me to stay true to myself, earn each day of my life, reevaluate what is important, discover and pursue my passions and offer me the opportunity to help others.

Hopefully, you all can learn some of these lessons without having to be diagnosed with a chronic or terminal illness.

It's time for all of us to wake up—live life, change our mindset, embrace all the possibilities that lie within us and live it up—hell yeah!

CHAPTER 37

LESSONS ON GRATITUDE WITH OPRAH

APRIL 17, 2012

I t's been a whirlwind of activity since arriving in Toronto but the event everyone is talking about is Monday's visit to Oprah's Lifeclass—The Tour. Oprah was filming her show live in Toronto and we had tickets thanks to the fabulous Auntie Cole.

When I discovered Oprah would be filming in Toronto the same week I was visiting, I immediately went online to try and get tickets. Unfortunately all the shows were sold out. But I threw the idea out to Auntie Cole anyway, knowing she was the queen of pulling rabbits out of her ass. Lo and behold, she made some calls and the next day we had two tickets to the show!

The theme of the show was *gratitude*—a perfect theme for my life these days, for all of our lives every single day. There were lessons about releasing expectations, finding joy in the seemingly mundane beauty of day-to-day life, how to instill gratitude in our children, finding ways to be grateful even during life's rough moments and how living life from a place of gratitude can make a monumental shift in the way you experience and perceive your existence.

One of the lessons that stuck with me is the importance of not letting one single solitary event define your whole life. I know I cannot let breast cancer, or my mom's death, overtake me or become my entire life. I'm so much more than that. We all are.

I know that living from a place of gratitude is one of the big reasons my scans were so successful last week. I know I must never lose sight of all that I have to be grateful for. Yes, life can totally suck at times. But who promised it wouldn't? Life is full of suffering. But it is also full of joy and beauty. And there is value in all our life experiences if we are open to looking for it and receiving it.

What am I grateful for today? I'm grateful for this time in Toronto to be with all my amazing friends, for the joy on Miss M's face when she plays and dances around with her BFF, Miss K, for the sunshine, for not having to do chemo and for the love I continue to receive from family, friends and even strangers all over the world.

What are you grateful for today?

CHAPTER 38

HOME SWEET HOME OHIO

APRIL 22, 2012

We have returned from our fabulous week in Toronto and it's good to be home. I'm detoxing from the chemo and my body is changing. I'm regaining energy. There's no more nausea, no more leg pains or head pains. I'm feeling healthy. It makes the remaining meds, falling off fingernails and bald patches on my head so much easier to deal with.

I finally have a few moments to really think about the results of my scans and process the good news.

While I know how amazing the news is, I still want to understand what this really means. *Is my cancer in remission? Does surgery now make sense? Is this just a small success amongst a long path of turmoil? Or is this a miraculous—cancer is now almost gone—cure sort of thing? Are the results a big deal, or a REALLY big deal?*

My relief is also interwoven with a lot of disbelief. *Can all the cancer that spread throughout my body, lymph nodes and bones really be gone? After just three months of chemo and a radical change in lifestyle and attitude? How long does this last? How long can I keep the cancer at bay? What exactly does this all mean?*

When I try to find information online about others like me I don't come up with much. Instead, I keep finding page-upon-page about the grim prognosis for Stage 4 patients—average survival rate of 18-24 months, treatment with no intention of curing the disease and focus on pain management.

Please…do not remind me!

It's so depressing reading all that crap. I know the odds are not in my favor. I don't need to be constantly reminded of the fact. *Why do I even read it?*

I know that no one can predict what path my disease will take. Just like all of our paths—the future is unknown. All I can do is recognize that right now, I feel good. Right now, my scans are clear. Right now, I don't have to do chemo. All I have is right now.

As my Zen calendar said today, "There is no enlightenment outside of daily life." This is it.

Our last night in Toronto, we went out for Chinese food. At the end of the meal we got our fortune cookies. I couldn't believe what mine said: "You will become an accomplished writer."

It's funny because as I got older I swore I would NEVER be a writer (or any kind of artist for that matter). I wanted a "real" job with a steady paycheck. Coming from a family of artists I knew firsthand the struggle of trying to be an artist for a living—and there was no way I was going that route. The fortune cookie got me thinking about my passion for the written word and what is really important.

I find that since the diagnosis I ask the "big questions" of myself a lot more often. My life is truly a gift—as are all our lives—and I feel this new drive to figure out who I want to be, what I want from life and to make my remaining years the best possible.

Be sure to keep asking the big questions.

CHAPTER 39

SPIRITED MATTERS

MAY 3, 2012

I'm counting down the hours till Miss M and I hit the road for Nashville. Looking forward to five quality days with my outspoken cousin, her sweet-as-honey husband, their five boys and my talented aunt.

I'm also excited about going to church Nashville-style. Last time we were in town we went to a service and I truly had a magical experience—tears flowed, bodies were swaying and Miss M was dancing—it was so moving. My one request for this trip was to go to church again.

I've been thinking a lot about spirituality, faith and religion lately. The breast cancer is demanding that of me. But even before that, hubby and I were feeling the pull to get more in touch with our spiritual sides.

To be clear, neither hubby nor I have ever really attended church as adults. Hubby grew up quasi Catholic, showing up at church for a holiday here and there. I was raised by two hippie artist parents who let me decide what religion I wanted to be. So hubby and I actually going to church on a regular basis would be a pretty big deal.

My mom did expose me to her love of Buddhism from an early age and instilled in me much of the wisdom without me even realizing it. I always tell the story of how she would bring me to the beach as a child and then suggest we just sit in silence, appreciate the view and not talk to each other for 20 minutes. I realize now that she was sowing the seeds for my meditation practice. She gave me my first zafu (meditation cushion) when I went off to college at age 17. I was so not ready to use it, but I kept it with me—move after move after move. At age 28 I was finally ready to embrace my Buddhist self. Hubby and I had a Buddhist wedding ceremony in San Francisco and I've been trying to stick to a relatively steady meditation practice ever since.

Today I'm so thankful to my mom for giving me this gift. I credit meditation with a lot of my ability to stay calm, centered and healthy—especially with everything that's happened over the last few years and this crazy breast cancer diagnosis.

At tonight's support group for young women with breast cancer, one of the other ladies commented to me that I seemed so positive. I think some people are surprised at the idea of being positive or happy when you've been handed a diagnosis of late stage cancer. But I think when you're grounded in a strong foundation of spirituality, community and faith, anything is possible.

It doesn't matter what religion you are. If you believe there is something bigger than yourself then you have an amazing resource to tap into. Whether you do it through prayer, song, being in nature, meditation—it don't matter. From the day I was diagnosed, I have appealed to the Universe and my mom's spirit to help me through this. And so far, they have.

CHAPTER 40

ZEN KOANS AND BIBLE PACKAGES

MAY 8, 2012

Riverboat Ridin' at Opreyland Resort

B̲ack home today from trip #2 on our "Summer Love Tour of Gratitude and Thanks." We had an absolute blast in Nashville. And yes, we made it to church on Sunday—as requested.

And that, too, was magical. Within the first five minutes the tears were flowing. With the soulful gospel music and all the love in the room I just couldn't stop myself. Then I thought, *Why even try to stop myself? Just let it out.* So I did. I cried, I sang, I smiled at my neighbors, thought about my mom and danced around with Miss M in my arms.

The sermon itself was just what I needed—a lesson in persever-ance, never giving up hope, finding the answers within yourself and recognizing your own power. I'm realizing that the passages in the Bible are just like Zen koans—big lessons stuffed in metaphorical and ambiguous little packages for us to figure out and incorporate.

The day after church I learned about the death of Amy Rauch Neilson, a fellow blogger, terrific writer, mom, wife and Stage 4 breast cancer warrior. She passed away on May 6, 2012 at the age of 43—way too young.

I thought of the sermon at church and questioned why another fabulous woman was taken away. I wondered why some die and some live. *How does this get decided? Do we have any control?* Again, I was forced to face the severity of my situation. I'm going to lose a lot of warriors in this journey. This sucks.

It's such a weird place to be, stuck in between two worlds. Watching fellow soldiers go down while still clinging to the belief that I will be the miracle. *But why me?*

Cancer is truly forcing me to live with a "beginner's mind," as Suzuki Roshi would say—no assumptions, no judgements, just pure wonder and lots of questions. There are no attachments to life being a certain way, just the here and now, the present moment, a challenge to live by my ideals and practice what I preach.

Cancer is a teacher, some twisted Zen koan that I have to figure out. All I know is that in this moment, I feel good. Today was a good day. And I'm praying for many more.

CHAPTER 41

CONTEMPLATING MOTHERHOOD

MAY 14, 2012

The miracle of my birth. October 25, 1974

Okay, I have to come clean. There is a new Procter & Gamble commercial that makes me cry EVERY time I watch it. It's about being a mom. The tag line is, "The hardest job in the world is the best job in the world. Thank you, mom." It captures the pure love, pride and endless devotion that moms all over the world give to their kids.

As moms, our days are often filled with endless tasks. We put our children's needs above our own. We tirelessly take care of all the details. We are our children's #1 cheerleaders. We are devoted and strong.

Oftentimes, a lot of what we do goes unnoticed. There are plenty of days when I feel that all my hard work goes unappreciated. But then there are moments when Miss M cuddles up with me and says, "I love you mommy" or offers to kiss my boo-boos, or gives me that special look that she gives to no one else but me. And I remember what it's all about.

Being a mom is often super emotional for me because I don't have my own mother to turn to anymore. Every time I have a special moment or adventure with Miss M it makes me think of my mom and all the special adventures we had together—overnights to funky little B&B's across Nova Scotia, dancing together at family functions, traveling to different places and seeing new things. As a daughter—and an only child—our relationship was especially close. We had an almost spiritual connection, an intuitive knowing, an unbreakable bond.

While I'm thankful for the 36 years we had together, I would have loved to have had more. I still can't believe she's gone.

And this is why I must continue my fight—for Miss M and for my mom.

I cannot give up. I cannot let down my guard. I must do everything in my power to stay on this earth as long as I can, to watch Miss M grow, to guide her, cheer her on and love her unconditionally.

Make sure your mom knows how much you love her and appreciate all that she does. Treasure the moments you have together. Do it now. Don't wait.

CHAPTER 42

A GIFT FOR MISS M

MAY 18, 2012

Great news arrived today—I DO NOT have the BRAC1 or BRAC2 gene mutation! *WooHoo!* It's one less thing for me to worry about and great news for both Miss M and me.

It decreases the risk that Miss M will develop breast, ovarian and other types of cancer. A woman who inherits the *BRCA1* or *BRCA2* gene is about five times more likely to develop breast cancer than a woman who doesn't have such a mutation. Many women who test positive for the gene even choose to get their breasts removed when they don't have breast cancer as a preventative and cautionary measure. I'm so glad Miss M won't have to face those same decisions.

Regardless, Miss M still has to face the possibility that she may develop cancer. Everyone has to face that possibility.

I stand by my beliefs that cancer risk is not just about genes. It's about harmful chemicals that we ingest on an everyday basis, the unhealthy, overly processed and nutrient void diets that most people consume, the toxic levels of stress in our society and the unforeseen tragedies that inhibit our ability to stay healthy. No one is immune.

I still think about how all of this will impact her in the years to come. *What's it like to grow up knowing your parent is sick and may die at any time?* That's some pretty heavy shit.

Even now, at age two (almost three), she says and does things that are not the "norm" for kids her age—she asks to help sort my vitamins and supplements each week into my days-of-the-week pillbox, assumes every appointment I go to is a doctor's visit (which I guess isn't too far from the truth) and always has to be conscious of my "boo-boos"—no grabbing my neck because she might mess up the line from my port or resting her head on certain parts of my chest because it hurts.

I guess this is just how life is for a kid whose parent has cancer (or any other disease for that matter). For the most part, she and I continue to live our lives and have fun together, despite the fact that the cancer is always there.

I never thought I wanted to be a stay-at-home mom but now I cannot imagine going back to work before she starts school and missing out on all these precious moments with her. I often think about how I'd just accepted a job offer in November, the week before I was diagnosed. My fingerprinting was scheduled mere hours after my mammogram (that I was convinced was going to be fine). Then the doctors told me it might not be the best idea to start a brand new full-time job right about now. So I didn't.

In essence, cancer—both my mom's and my own—has enabled me to stay home with Miss M and given me the gift of being intimately involved in the early years of her life. It's funny how I see all these gifts around me now that I didn't see before.

Take a look around and find the gifts. They may be hard to find, but they're there.

CHAPTER 43

HUNGER FOR LIFE

MAY 22, 2012

Ages ago my cousin Jamie told me I had to read the book, "The Hunger Games." After hearing the premise of the story, I thought, *Oh, how barbaric and depressing! There's no way I'm reading that.* Flashforward to a few weeks ago when my good friend, Sam, tossed the book my way. It sat on my shelf for a while then I finally picked it up. And let me tell you, I could not put that book down. While it was just as disturbing as I thought it would be, I still got hooked and devoured the whole thing in a few days.

I started thinking about the parallels between my life and the kids in the hunger games—how I've been thrown into the arena with cancer and am now in a constant battle for my life. I too must stay strong and healthy, mentally and spiritually fit, train hard to stay one step ahead, gather as much information as possible and develop strategies to outsmart my enemy. Cancer is devious and cunning and stands poised to attack at any time. I need to constantly be on alert—ready. If I give cancer any opportunity to take over my body and my life, it will.

The one thing I know for sure is that my strategy does not involve sitting back and waiting to see what the cancer will do. When your life is on the line you must be proactive, so I'm doing everything I possibly can to beat this beast down and keep it down. I don't care if it's been proven or not. If there's a chance it can help me, I'm willing to consider it. *Why the fuck not?*

Why not do whatever it takes to keep living? Why not question your doctors? Why not research all possible solutions? Why not get a second, third and even fourth opinion? Why not change your diet? Why not consider doing things a little differently?

I want to live. I have a newfound hunger for life. And I'm willing to do whatever it takes to stay in the game.

CHAPTER 44

FEELING THE VIBE

MAY 30, 2012

Where do I even begin?

My beloved NYC—travel adventure #3 of our "Summer Love Tour." This city is such a whirlwind of energy. It just sucks you up into it. It's been non-stop fabulous fun since Miss M and I arrived. We've hung out at Washington Square Park, reunited with family and friends, took a side trip to Long Island, attended an amazing baby shower for my cousin upstate, and today— the icing on the cake—a purely joyful afternoon at Coney Island for Miss M's NYC birthday celebration.

It brings so much joy to my heart seeing how Miss M loves being here—settling into the vibe of the city, dancing her ass off to the house music on the boardwalk at Coney Island, yabbering on about all the different subway trains she wants to ride. She is a New Yorker. She was born here. It will always have a piece of her soul as it does mine.

And being here made today, the second anniversary of my mom's passing, easier to bear. It's a weird day. You don't really want to "celebrate," per se. But the day cannot go unrecognized. All day long she's been with me—in my thoughts, in my prayers, in my meditation session, in the James Taylor music that came on the radio. I know she's helping me on this journey. But I still wish she were here in person, alive, to hold me and cheer me through it all. She was always my biggest cheerleader. I miss you, mom.

What also makes this anniversary easier to bear is the incredible support I continue to receive. Last week the Bowen Island community came out in full force and threw one of the most amazing benefits ever. Thank you Bowen!

Bowen Island is a special place. Rumor has it that the island has healing properties. I believe it. When hubby and I moved there at the end of 2009 to care for my mom we had no idea what to expect. What we found there was a genuine community, a bunch of really friendly people who look out for one another. There is a sense of pride with untouched rainforest and beaches everywhere. Hubby and I even had an ocean view from our deck. It was glorious! My parents knew that Bowen was special. That's why they moved there. And I couldn't think of a better place for them to have settled down.

When my mom was diagnosed with biliary cancer the entire island came out to support us. An amazing benefit was orchestrated. Special healthy cancer-fighting meals were prepared and delivered—constantly. Helpful books were dropped off. Support was offered in every which way imaginable. And now to see the island coming out *yet* again to rally behind my family is unbelievable. The love and support just never ends.

So thank you, Bowen. Having the support and love of so many people really does help me feel like I can triumph over cancer. It makes it easier to face the day, easier to heal. It gives me strength to continue fighting and to live out the essence of my name—Luanna—Graceful Woman Warrior.

And thank you NYC, for bringing me so much joy, allowing me to forget about the cancer for a few days, sparking a light inside Miss M and putting a smile on her face and providing the perfect backdrop for life to unfold.

Grandpa and the Wonder Wheel at Coney Island

CHAPTER 45

THROWING CURVE BALLS

JUNE 8, 2012

There's been some new thoughts about my treatment plan.

On Wednesday I met with my doctor at Sloan-Kettering in NYC. The big topic of conversation was surgery, something not normally considered for metastatic patients. In certain situations like mine, people are saying maybe we should reconsider. When the cancer has suddenly retreated and the only thing left is a piece of the primary tumor, maybe it would help to remove it.

Do I get the mastectomy? Should I take out my ovaries too since my cancer is estrogen positive? What about a full-on hysterectomy? The damn Tamoxifen may cause uterine cancer so why not get the uterus removed while they're in there as a precautionary measure? But if I have no breasts, no uterus, no ovaries, no more female parts—what does that make me? What the hell would that feel like? Can my body handle all that?

In addition, the problem with surgery is that it will be a four-month long ordeal. With a mastectomy, reconstructive surgery and possible ovary removal, the recovery would be long and I'd have to return to Sloan-Kettering weekly for follow-ups with the doctors and surgeons. This means I'd have to live in NYC for four months and disrupt little Miss M's life—not to mention hubby's and mine. I'd need to find someone to help me care for Miss M on those days when I can't get out of bed or lift a 30-lb. munchkin out of the bathtub. It's a lot to consider and orchestrate.

I set up an appointment to go to the Block Center for Integrative Cancer Treatment outside of Chicago. I really want to find a team that's knowledgeable about both Eastern and Western medicine and how to combine the two. They're all about diet, exercise and the mind-body connection, while also promoting traditional Western treatments like surgery and chemotherapy when necessary. I'm hoping this will be the place that truly integrates all the pieces of my treatment and helps me make a decision on whether or not to do surgery.

It just goes to show that you truly cannot predict the future. As my mom always said, "The only constant in life is change." Just when you think you're getting things figured out—life throws you a curve ball. *Craziness!*

CHAPTER 46

THE ROOT OF IT ALL

JUNE 17, 2012

Having a terrific time out east with all my favorite people. This past week has been so chock-full of memorable moments and good times I don't even know where to start.

Let's see, there was the amazing Crosby, Stills & Nash concert Friday night, Miss M's first slumber party at her buddy Jilly's house (which when asked what she did at the sleepover, Miss M proudly exclaimed, "I slept!"), the much-needed days at the beach, meditating on the movement of the ocean's waves and watching Miss M frolic in the sand, Miss M's much-anticipated ride on Auntie M's new horsy and the great party for my cousin's high school graduation that allowed me to not only celebrate him, but to personally thank so many of the people who were at my Massachusetts benefit.

Then there was Miss M's Brazilian Birthday BBQ yesterday (her third birthday party since her actual birthday!). Just having the opportunity to be with my closest peeps was incredible—to feed them and thank them for all they've done, laugh and smile, create new memories, take joy in our children—the next generation—watch them frolic and their connections develop.

This trip has re-solidified my and hubby's desire to move back east. This is where we belong. I know somehow, someway, we'll get back here and be closer to the family and our roots.

In the meantime, it's back to Ohio tomorrow—which, of course, is bittersweet. It'll feel good to get back into the routine. Miss M is psyched to see her friends and sleep in her own bed. My body is craving my daily dose of green juice. But we're going to miss our NYC and Massachusetts peeps so much.

Until next time...

CHAPTER 47

MY CROSS TO BEAR

JUNE 22, 2012

Everyone has a cross to bear. I said this to my aunt the other day. Mine just happens to be breast cancer. For others, it may be the struggle to get pregnant or have children… Or those stuck in toxic relationships… Or those surrounded by never ending family feuds or people who are not supportive or loving…

We all have something we are stuck with, some troubling aspect of our lives. And while it's super easy to allow the difficulties in life to become our life, it's so important for me not to let myself go there.

This is my cross to bear. I have breast cancer. I will always be a breast cancer patient. Even when I'm given the stamp of NED (no evidence of disease)—notice I said "when" and not "if"—even then, I'll still have to get scanned and examined on the regular, live with the fear that the cancer may come back and question each and every ache and pain and worry it's cancer.

Who's to say one person's cross is worse than another's? Every cross is different. And they are all difficult. They all suck. They all bring pain. Yet our crosses can also force us to ask big questions, re-evaluate priorities and make a commitment to living a fuller life. Amidst the turmoil, we can try to make peace with our crosses, figure out why that particular cross is ours to bear in the first place, understand the lessons contained in the suffering and use it all as an opportunity to grow, learn and discover who we truly are.

To all those out there with a cross to bear, I feel your pain. We're all in this together. As my dad, author Spider Robinson, said, "Shared pain is lessened, shared joy, increased."

So let's all keep sharing.

CHAPTER 48

ARMED WITH NEW INFORMATION

JULY 8, 2012

The big news coming out of my visit to the Block Center is the decision to get surgery. Yep, I've decided to get a mastectomy. Both the team in Chicago and the team in NYC are suggesting I have surgery to remove the final remaining tumor in my left breast. The doctors at the Block Center cited new research, saying surgery does help improve lifespan in metastatic breast cancer patients—so I'm going for it.

I have to say I'm so glad I went to the Block Center. It was great to get another opinion to balance out Ohio and NYC. Of course, when I told my NYC doctor about the visit, she said, "The Block Center? Never heard of it. Just be cautious. Some of these places drain people of their last pennies and offer nothing more than you would get at a reputable hospital." A typical cynical New Yorker response. Interestingly enough, when I told Dr. K about the visit his response was something along the lines of, "Interesting. Let me know if you find out anything new that is helpful. I'd love to hear about different approaches." This is why I love Dr. K.

I finished reading Dr. Block's book, "Life Over Cancer," right before my trip to Chicago and absolutely loved it. His team was phenomenal. I not only got confirmation that surgery is the way to go but also got reassurance I'm on the right path. The entire staff seemed knowledgeable, kind and caring. They assured me there are a number of great options to treat the cancer if it ever does come back. They made sure to convey how amazing it was that I responded so well to treatment. Dr. Block himself said there must be a guardian angel watching over me. I replied, "Yep, that would be my mom."

The only way I'm able to continue on this path of healing and miracles is because of the generosity and support of all of you. I can't even express how grateful I am that I don't have to worry about how I'm going to pay my medical bills, or Miss M's daycare bills, or worry about not getting the best medical care. I can just take care of me, take care of my family, focus on getting better and make decisions about my health that are smart and informed.

Thank you everyone. Your support is helping keep me alive. I am blessed.

CHAPTER 49

SURGICAL CONSIDERATIONS

JULY 27, 2012

Surgery—yuck. I hate medical procedures.

Truthfully, when I think about going through with the mastectomy it kind of terrifies me—the pain, the anesthesia, the scars and the constant reminder of the fact I have cancer every time I get dressed or look down at my chest.

Just the other day I was chatting with a woman at Miss M's preschool who is from Long Island (immediate connection) and a cancer survivor. I asked her if the whole cancer thing gets any easier with time. She told me it's impossible to ever forget you've had cancer. Even though she was diagnosed 20 years ago she's still reminded of the fact on a daily basis. She explained that her body is a constant reminder—from the body parts that were either added or taken away, to the scars—both physical and mental. And then there's the hair that grew back differently. She said the cancer just becomes a part of who you are—the new you, the new life.

Tonight I was re-introduced to the blog of a young Boston woman, Bridget Spence, who was diagnosed at age 21 with Stage 4 breast cancer right out of the gate—just like me. Reading other Stage 4 breast cancer blogs is always a mixed bag for me. Part of me really loves the sense of understanding and reassurance I get from reading others' stories. But the other part hates the reminder of how much this is going to suck, that the road is long (Bridget has had eight different surgeries) and the fact that having breast cancer will never completely go away.

It seems for most Stage 4 ladies the cancer comes in waves. It pushes up onto the shore and then it retreats. So just like Bridget, I live my life in three-four month increments—making plans but never knowing if I'll be able to keep them, doing things when I feel good and trying to lay low when I don't. Silently, in my head, I think about how much time I have left. *Do I need to take that trip to India now? Or can it wait a few years? Do I need to keep wearing anti-aging cream? Should I keep saving for retirement? Or cash in my 401K?*

A few nights ago hubby opened up about how sad he is—sad that our lives are forever changed, sad that I have to go through surgery and be in pain and sad at the thought that Miss M might lose her mom.

Of course I'm sad, too. But I've gotten really good at detaching myself from the sadness, just putting one foot in front of the other and trying to enjoy the moment because who knows how many moments I have left. I don't want to waste them. I don't want to be asleep when I can be awake. I don't want to obsess about cleaning when I can be enjoying time with Miss M.

I flew to NYC to meet with my new surgeons, both of whom were recommended by a friend of mine. My oncology surgeon, Dr. B seemed kind, caring, flexible and honest. My plastic surgeon, Dr. F, is a top dog on Park Avenue with a great sense of humor who appears genuine and committed. All in all, it's a great team.

Despite my own reservations and fears about having surgery (that prompted a minor teary meltdown in the plastic surgeon's office), I'm feeling a lot better about the whole thing after meeting with them.

The procedure will involve having my left breast surgically removed and tissue expanders put in. I'll be in the hospital for a few days and then go home to lay low and recoup. Of course, where exactly I'll be recouping is still yet to be decided. I imagine I'll have to stay in NYC for at least two-four weeks.

After that, I return once every two weeks to have the skin on my breast slowly stretched out to the desired size. Then we do yet another (minor) surgery to remove the expander and put the implant in, as well as do any "touch ups" to the right breast to make sure the two breasts match.

There is also the question of what to do about my lymph nodes. We have no definitive way of knowing if there still is cancer in the lymph nodes closest to my breast until they cut me open. Dr. B is asking me to consider either a sentinal lymph node biopsy or an axillary lymph node dissection to test the tissue and remove any cancerous nodes. Before any of this can start, I have to go in for yet another set of scans (MRI, PET, and bone scan).

Needless to say, I've got a lot of thinking and research to do— about the surgery, the reconstruction and where I'm going to live immediately following my surgery as well as who is going to take care of me and Miss M.

I am doing my best to keep living each day as it comes, focusing on the here and now. I'm trying to remain open to what life has to offer and not get stressed out about the things I can't control.

This new approach seems to be working really well so far. And it sure is making life a hell of a lot more fun to live, too.

My beloved NYC-Across from Astoria Park

CHAPTER 50

BEAUTY IS EVERYWHERE

AUGUST 7, 2012

Miss M and I have arrived in Vancouver—our final stop on our "Summer Love Tour."

After a hellish flight including a six-hour layover and an arrival time of 2:00 am which translated into 5:00 am Ohio time (thank God Auntie Cole was there to pick us up), we are now happily settled at grandpa's house on Bowen Island. The sun is shining (a rarity around these parts), the air smells delicious, the birds are chirping and the views of the ocean and mountains are breathtakingly beautiful. It feels good to be back.

Miss M and I are overjoyed to be spending time with some of our favorite people in the Pacific Northwest—collecting and giving hugs, catching up on life and saying thank you. In my short time living on Bowen Island, I managed to forge some pretty terrific friendships. It feels great to be back again, picking up right where we left off. The Bowen community is truly a special one—one I feel privileged to be a part of.

Bowen also feels good on a physical level. My body is relaxed here. My soul is comforted. Nature surrounds you wherever you go—the salt air, the ebb and flow of the waves, the glorious mountains, walking through the rainforest and listening to the birds. I don't need to set aside time for meditation while I'm here. Life on Bowen feels like one never ending meditation session. *Aaahhhh....*

This week also brought some serious emotional upheavals—including the loss of yet another young mother to cancer, Vancouver resident and friend, Charline Leith. Charline was only 45. She was a wife, mom to two beautiful boys, sister, beloved friend and so much more. She was taken way too soon.

I attended the celebration of her life along with 300 people. Charline and I were both diagnosed with Stage 4 cancer at the same time (hers a recurrence of ovarian cancer, mine an initial diagnosis of breast cancer). To see her go only nine months later was really hard to swallow. Even though we were never close friends I felt connected to her because we both were in the same "late stage cancer club." We both have young kids. She read my blog. Auntie Cole kept us informed about each other's ups and downs in our respective cancer journeys.

I was unsure about going to the service. I had some definite sur-vivor's guilt going on. *Would people be upset to see me there? To see me living after Charline was gone?* Losing Charline was also a reminder that my cancer could roar to life again, ravage my body and take me away.

The latest news on the cancer front is that my most recent echo-cardiogram showed a decrease in my heart functioning. Any lower and I may want to consider discontinuing the Herceptin. For now, Dr. K says not to worry—so I'm trying not to.

Dr. K also mentioned that if I remain tumor free after surgery we may be able to stop the Herceptin anyway. Although metastatic patients are often on Herceptin indefinitely, earlier stage breast cancer patients usually take the drug for just one year post-surgery. Apparently now that I have responded so well to treatment, I could possibly be treated in a similar fashion.

The other news is that my breast surgery is scheduled at Lenox Hill Hospital in NYC in five weeks. Between now and then I have to do a ton of prep for the surgery, including a PET scan, bone scan, MRI, EKG, complete physical and extensive blood work. All of this will be done in Ohio when I get back at the end of the month. Plus, I still have to coordinate all the logistics—travel plans, care schedules, hubby's paperwork to request medical leave, recovery and aftercare. I continue to trust that the details will work themselves out, that the Universe (and my mom) will help me pull it all together.

People often ask how I continue to stay positive while living with metastatic breast cancer and the ever-lurking fear of death that accompanies it. What I'm finding is that the world is full of positive people living and thriving despite debilitating diseases, heart wrenching upsets and unfortunate circumstances. I'm not exactly sure how we do it. We just do it.

Tomorrow is not guaranteed, so I'm making a conscious effort to make the most out of each and every day, notice the beauty that is everywhere around me and appreciate the hell out of it.

CHAPTER 51

LET THE SCANS BEGIN

AUGUST 26, 2012

Tomorrow commences the scanning ritual I must now endure every four months for the rest of my life—except this time around, I've got some extra scans thrown in for my surgery prep. It's so freakin' time-consuming.

My schedule tomorrow includes a 10:00 am injection (for my afternoon bone scan), an 11:00 am psychotherapy appointment (in another town), a 1:00 pm bone scan and then a routine EKG and chest x-ray. *Insane!*

The week continues with an MRI and PET scan. Then I have an appointment to visit my dermatologist for my six-month check-in to make sure the very early stage melanoma I had in 2008 does not come back.

On top of this I'm trying to coordinate all the details and paperwork for my upcoming surgery in NYC. It's never ending.

I don't even know how I'm feeling about the surgery. I haven't had time to just sit and think about what it'll be like. Maybe I'm purposefully trying NOT to think about what it'll be like—how scary this is, how much pain I'll be in, how incapacitated I'll be…

Instead, I just keep focusing on the here and now—what I have to get done in the next 24 hours, fun moments and memories that are constantly evolving around me, the beauty in the sunset, of my daughter, in celebrating my nine-year wedding anniversary and of being back home in Ohio sleeping in my own bed next to my husband.

It's so much more fun to think about the beauty that's all around me in the present moment than to think about the pain and stress of my upcoming surgery.

At my last Reiki appointment, Renee brought me the tarot card of Power or Strength. Reading the power card refocused my energy and reminded me to continue on my path. It spoke to my unlimited power as a spiritual being and how keeping my body, mind, soul and spirit balanced can help me overcome any obstacle in life.

As long as I do my best to stay balanced—take care of myself, relax, have fun, eat well, exercise, meditate—I can deal with everything else. It's only when I'm not attending to my basic needs and internal balance that I get off kilter, feel stressed, have all sorts of pains and get overly anxious about everything.

Now when I feel myself veering off course and reaching my tipping point, the new Terri makes a conscious effort to re-balance as quickly as possible. It's not easy, but I'm trying.

Maybe it's time we all take a step back and assess how balanced we truly are and try to realign ourselves before we get so unbalanced that we topple over.

As I go through the next few weeks I know that remaining balanced is key. I also know that through my connection to "The Universe," I have the power to make it through anything. We all do.

CHAPTER 52

WATING GAME

SEPTEMBER 5, 2012

I had a slight breakdown in the MRI machine today.

Part of my work in therapy is to allow myself to feel emotions. So, when I felt panicked, sad and angry in the MRI machine, I just went with it.

There I was, splayed out in superman position, boobs expertly positioned to drop into two little cups, arms totally straight so I wouldn't kink the injection line, trying not to put too much pressure on my chemo port—which is hard to do when you're lying flat on your chest—and then the jackhammers start. *Oh boy.* They give you headphones with really loud music to help drown out the noise. But it's really hard to overpower the sound of jackhammers. Half way through, they pump the injection line with some awful chemical that turns my mouth to rust. I'm doing my best not to move at all because if I do I'll have to start the whole process over again—and I REALLY don't want that.

So I just started to cry—it was either that or a full-on panic attack. I tried to do my counting meditation—counting up to ten and back again, imagining myself on a beautiful beach, drink in hand—but in the end, I just let the tears fall and the emotions come.

These are the days it sucks to have breast cancer.

Tomorrow I find out the results of my scans. The results determine a whole host of things, most importantly whether or not surgery is still an option. As long as the cancer hasn't grown or spread since my last scan in April, I'm good to go for the mastectomy.

What am I doing to stave off all the "scanxiety?" I just try to be in the moment—spending time with my girlfriends, dancing in the rain with Miss M, going on mini retreats with hubby, making time for the people I love, reading books for pleasure (instead of just books about cancer), watching trashy reality TV, trying to be in the here and now and not allow my mind to wander to the place of "what if."

One thing I've noticed lately is that by taking care of myself—making fun a priority, meditating, listening to my heart, honoring my spirit, communing with nature, working on my mental mess—I'm finding important lessons everywhere I look. For the longest time I couldn't see these lessons. I was too caught up in the stress of life, getting through the day, being there for everyone else and not taking the time to step back, pause and see what was all around me. Now I see the lessons everywhere—in my everyday tasks, the trees and the sky and even in the shows I watch on TV (yes, even the trashy ones!)

This past weekend hubby and I went to Harmony Farm for a couples' massage and mini-retreat to celebrate our nine-year anniversary. While there I took a walk through their beautiful brick and stone labyrinth. As I slowly made my way along the path to the center of the labyrinth I noticed how each time I looked too far ahead I lost my balance and went off the path. I realized the key to staying centered was to just focus on what was right in front of me. I realized how that was a metaphor for life. When I try to look too far ahead into the future it gets me nowhere. To stay balanced I must remain in the moment and focus on today— and maybe tomorrow—but not much further than that.

In my own path to healing I'm reminded again and again just how important it is to be still, quiet the mind, leave space for the lessons to appear and try not to look too far ahead.

CHAPTER 53

THE NEWS IS IN

SEPTEMBER 6, 2012

The news is both good and bad.

First the good news—my bone scan was clean and the PET scan showed no evidence of cancer in the bones, lymph nodes, organs, lungs, brain or anywhere else in my body. All the cancer is still contained in my left breast. So it looks like we're good to go for surgery next week. *Yay!*

The bad news is that the cancer in my left breast has grown. Both of the original tumors doubled in size since April. Plus, there is now a new tumor that has taken up residence in between the two old ones. This was definitely not what I wanted to hear. It's taken me all day to process the news.

Although I'm genuinely happy to find out the cancer did not spread again, I was totally freaked out and upset by the fact that it's still growing. To me, the cancer growth meant something wasn't working. *What was missing? What were we doing wrong? What could we be doing better? Maybe I need to eat better, exercise more, be more vigilant, cut out the occasional wine drinking, stop straying from my prescribed diet,*

*be more conscious of my defenses and entrenched behavioral patterns and
figure out the lessons that the cancer is here to teach me.*

These thoughts tumbled through my head all day long. I did a
lot of crying and a lot of processing. Thank god I also had my therapy appointment this afternoon and my breast cancer support group
tonight—both of which allowed me the chance to process further, feel
what I needed to feel and ultimately end up in a better place. Turns out
I'm actually getting better at feeling the feelings instead of just stuffing
them down.

At the end of the day I do recognize that the good in the situation
outweighs the bad. Next week I'll go in for surgery and get all these
tumors removed from my body. Going forward I'll continue to do the
necessary work to keep the cancer at bay.

Thanks to everyone for all the positive and supportive comments,
emails, phone and text messages. I feel the love and it is a beautiful thing.

CHAPTER 54

SURGERY TIME

SEPTEMBER 12, 2012

Tomorrow is my big surgery day.

I've got nervous energy coursing through my veins, random twinges of discomfort in my breast and this aching pain in the pit of my loins—like my lady parts know they're about to lose one of their own.

Miss M and I took a two-day long road trip from Ohio to Massachusetts, arriving at Auntie L's house late Monday night. Auntie L, Uncle M and the rest of my family have agreed to take care of Miss M while I'm in NYC for the surgery. God bless them. This morning I had to say goodbye to her. Knowing I won't see her for a full week—the longest we've ever been apart—adds more angst to my already anxiety full body. *Sigh...*

Thankfully I'm now safely in my beloved NYC, sitting in Astoria Park and looking out over the East River and the Manhattan skyline. It always feels so soothing and comforting to be here. NYC will always be home to me, the place I feel most comfortable, most at ease, most like myself.

In one hour hubby arrives and we get to spend one glorious day alone together in the city—wandering the streets, going out for dinner, maybe hitting up my favorite spot, Washington Square Park for some people watching and music—some quality time to enjoy each other and the city.

Interestingly, I just received an amazing text from hubby. He said on his first flight today he sat beside a woman named Jeanne (the same name as my mom) who is a Buddhist, dancer, and writer (just like my mom) and a fan of my dad's work. How about that for serendipitous events and reassuring messages from the Universe?

I know in my heart of hearts that my mom is watching over me—that the Universe's energy, which is in all of us and always surrounding us, is channeling good energy my way. I feel it radiating from the pores of the Big Apple, embracing me from afar with all the love and good energy you all are sending my way.

Thanks again to everyone for your support in this journey. I'm in the midst of a very difficult chapter in my life, but I know this too shall pass—as everything does.

CHAPTER 55

A SURGICAL SUCCESS STORY

SEPTEMBER 16, 2012

We did it! With the love and support of my husband, friends, family, and blog readers—not to mention my skillful surgeons—I made it through surgery successfully.

The day of the surgery itself is a total blur to me. I remember the prep, the chats with my surgeons and the anesthesiologist before I went into the OR and the doctors sticking up for my right to have my iPod during the procedure (despite some resistance from the nursing staff). I remember waking up and feeling like total crap, throwing up multiple times, the pain when they transferred me from the OR stretcher to my bed and the persistent nausea that clung to me for hours upon hours, preventing me from talking or even opening my eyes. I also remember the beauty of the sky outside my hospital window as the sun rose up and shone its light onto the magnificent architecture of the buildings across from me and I realized I wasn't nauseous any more. Hubby later told me he made sure to grab the bed closest to the window knowing I would want to see the Manhattan skyline when I finally came to. Thank you, my love!

I was told the surgery itself took about two and a half to three hours. The sentinel lymph node biopsy led them to remove just one lymph node that tested negative for cancer, reaffirming the scan findings that showed no more cancer in my lymph nodes. Thankfully, we didn't have to remove a ton of lymph nodes for testing, which means my chances of getting lymphodema down the road are pretty slim.

Now they're sending my breast tissue to the lab for testing. It's important to find out the make-up of the tumors—especially the new one that appeared since my last set of scans—so we can properly target any future treatments. Of the three tumors that were in my left breast, each could require a different targeted therapy.

I'll also be meeting with my plastic surgeon at some point this week. I saw him the morning after the surgery and he was very pleased with how everything went. For the next three to six months, I'll travel back to NYC every two weeks or so while we stretch the skin to the desired size for my new implant—which will require yet another (albeit less intense) surgery down the road.

Today I'm just happy that I'm feeling better and the pain is lessening. I still haven't looked at my chest (or what's left of it). I'm not quite ready for that yet. I've been crying a lot the last few days, just frustrated with this never ending cancer journey and so wanting to be done with it already, but realizing it will never truly be over.

On a positive note, the surgery has helped hubby and I grow closer and more secure in our love for one another. We both miss our darling Miss M like crazy. I don't know how I'm gonna wait another five whole days to see her, kiss her, smell her, hold her. But we're just so thankful that during this time she is surrounded by the love of some of her favorite people and that she's being well taken care of.

Again, I want to thank everyone for your healing prayers and encouragement. The day after my surgery I awoke to emails, texts and Facebook messages from all over the world wishing me well. It made me feel so loved and supported amidst the hell and pain of life immediately after my surgery. Thank you—really—thank you.

CHAPTER 56

HOW DO YOU PARENT THROUGH CANCER?

SEPTEMBER 25, 2018

Our first visit one week post-surgery at the Hope Lodge in NYC
Photo credit- Eryka Peskin

M iss M is a hot mess these days. She's angry. She's acting out. She's fussier than I've ever seen her. She's yelling and screaming and throwing things. She's glued to my side and constantly crying. She's going through a lot.

Hubby and I naturally assume the acting out is related to my absence—we were apart for almost ten days. I know it doesn't seem like much, but when you're a stay-at-home mom who is with your kid 24/7, even a few days can seem like forever. She knows I was at the doctor while I was away from her. She also knows that I have some serious "boo boos."

The few times she's been able to articulate why she's so mad, she's said, "Because mommy goes to the doctor a lot." It just breaks my heart.

We really don't know what to do. I know I'm not supposed to burden her with my problems, illness or pain. But even if I don't talk about it she knows. She senses what I'm going through. She sees that I'm not the same person I was a month ago. Miss M and I have spent practically every moment together since she was a baby. Our connection runs deep. And there's no way I can pretend that everything is normal—because it's not.

The evening of our first reunion post-surgery ended with her in hysterics when she found out I wasn't staying with her at Cousin J's that night. The next day she demanded that I sit beside her for the entire ten-hour drive back to Ohio. Since we got back, she's been glued to my side, looking for extra hugs, asking me to hold her, wanting lots of cuddle time. She's been fussy with her friends. Each time I tell her I can't do something I used to—like picking her up or holding her tight to my chest—she freaks out, starts crying and runs away to hide. Tonight she refused to sleep in her bed and demanded to sleep in our room, something she hasn't done in ages.

What's a mom to do? If I give in to her every demand, am I spoiling her? But with everything that she's been through doesn't she deserve a little spoiling? A little extra attention? A little extra love?

We are actively looking for a good therapist. Hubby and I—and even my dad who is staying with us to help during my recovery—are all at a loss for what to do. I would love to hear from other moms who parented young children while fighting a chronic illness. How did you make it through? What helped? How are your kids now?

In the end, I know we'll make it through this somehow. It just seems like a never ending journey sometimes. I'm so sick of cancer taking away my ability to be the fully engaged, energetic, active mom I used to be. We keep telling Miss M that mommy's gonna get better soon. But really, when will that be? It feels like every time I'm done with one piece of the treatment puzzle, there's another piece right behind waiting to fuck with my life. I'm so sick of it already!

I think I need to go eat a cookie.

CHAPTER 57

PARENTING THANKS

SEPTEMBER 27, 2012

A quick thank you to everyone who chimed in with their two cents. I found all your responses so helpful and comforting. Miss M is still flipping out and she's still upset more hours in the day than not, but I'm feeling bolstered by the new ideas and avenues you all suggested for us to explore.

I've struggled with not knowing how much to tell her—she is, after all, only three-years- old. After reading about all your experiences, I feel that it's okay to be honest with her (in three-year-old terms of course). The reality is I can't hide this from her, so why not keep it real? Let her know what's happening and what she can expect? Let her know I love her dearly and always will? Let her know it's ok to be mad, sad and frustrated?

I will continue to do my best to create a firm and loving holding environment for her, set limits, continue with our daily routines and surround her with people who care and love her unconditionally.

Mark, Elenore, Gwyneth, Jewel, and Joelyne—thank you for sharing your personal stories with me about navigating the ups and downs of living in a household with family illness. I'm touched by your candor and willingness to open up.

Lisa Marie, I love the Neufeld Institute site you forwarded to me. Their approach seems very much in line with my leanings toward attachment parenting.

Rhonda Lea, your words broke my heart—I'm so sorry you didn't receive the reassurance you needed as a child. After reading your comment I made it a point to tell Miss M she was in no way responsible for me having cancer and that nothing she says or does would make me sick. This elicited a big smile from her. Thank you!

And Lois, I couldn't agree more with your dad's wisdom: "When they are the most unlovable is when they need the most love." I will try to remember this when Miss M is at her worst and I'm at my wit's end.

This is an ongoing battle. We're all still adjusting to our new "normal." But I have faith that we'll make it through—in large part due to the beautiful support and guidance from all of you.

CHAPTER 58

BLOOD CLOTS, HOSPITAL STAYS AND NEW MEDICATIONS

OCTOBER 3, 2012

It's been one hell of a week.

Last Thursday I was scheduled to fly to NYC to meet with my plastic surgeon. Instead, I ended up in the hospital in Ohio with a blood clot in the lung (otherwise known as a pulmonary embolism). *Scary shit!*

In the days leading up to my hospitalization I'd been feeling pretty crappy but I just chalked it up to the cold I was fighting and side effects from the Herceptin. But things got worse. All of a sudden I was out of breath just reading bedtime stories to Miss M. I couldn't lie down on my back to go to sleep. It hurt like hell to take a deep breath. I had a persistent scratchy cough. I knew something was wrong.

We went to the local after-hours clinic to get it checked out. The doctor there said my lungs sounded okay but feared it may be a blood clot so he sent us to the emergency room. After a bunch of tests, some blood work and a very painful CT scan, it was confirmed that yes, there was indeed a blood clot in my lung. Luckily it was small and we caught it early. Immediately I was put on blood thinners and admitted to the hospital where I stayed for the next three days.

I never imagined I would be at risk for blood clots. I exercise daily. I don't smoke (anymore). I'm not overweight or sedentary. You never think these things will happen to you—until they do. Apparently, I have many of the risk factors for developing blood clots—a history of cancer, an intravenous port in my chest and recent surgery immediately followed by an extremely long drive from NYC to Ohio. So there ya go.

The good news—other than the obvious fact that I'm alive—is that Dr. K is taking me off both the Herceptin and Tamoxifen. This is great because I was just about to tell him I no longer wanted to take the Tamoxifen anyway.

The bad news is that I now have a whole new host of minor health issues to worry about. I'll be taking blood thinners daily for the next six months (maybe longer). The new meds don't seem to have any seriously scary side effects, but they do cause me to bruise all the time and put me at danger for excessive bleeding. I have to be über careful not to fall, get cut or hurt in any way. Even a strong bump or whack against a heavy object—or attack by an energetic three-year-old—can cause major internal bleeding that I may not even be aware of. If I was cautious before because of my surgery scars, now I feel like I should be wearing a protective suit everywhere I go.

Despite all these health issues I'm feeling pretty good. The blood thinners have taken away the pain and allowed me to breathe easy again. My energy is good. My appetite is fine. I'm healing from the mastectomy and gaining increased range of motion and strength in my left arm and chest every day.

Dr. K says I should be able to go to NYC next week to meet with my plastic surgeon. So that's the plan for now. But I haven't booked my ticket just yet.

I'm realizing (yet again) I can never truly predict what will happen from day-to-day. Any minute a new issue may arise and I'm having a difficult time adjusting.

This is not an easy journey. I'm pissed that this is my new normal. I'm sad that I can't just live my life in blissful ignorance. I'm still trying to figure out the lesson breast cancer has come to teach me. And I still have many days where I just feel sorry for myself and for my husband, daughter, family and friends.

But I'll never give up. And I'll never stop fighting. I will not let cancer ruin my life.

CHAPTER 59

TIME TO PULL MYSLEF OUT OF SADNESS

OCTOBER 21, 2012

The last couple of months have been a real struggle for me—the surgery, recovery, changes to my everyday routines and seasons, missing life in NYC and not loving life in Ohio, the blood clot in my lung, more hospital stays and doctor's visits, one highly emotional and unruly toddler and the lack of energy and low-level depression that takes up too much space in my head and makes me not want to do much of anything (including write). I also need to deal with the never ending medical research, complicated medical decisions, difficult acknowledging of painful, repressed feelings in therapy and the demands of being a cancer patient, mother, and wife.

And finally, there's the resistance to accepting that all of this is my new normal.

The ladies from my dad's online support group recently expressed concern because they hadn't seen a post from me. Was everything okay? Technically, yes. Life goes on. I'm breathing. I'm alive.

But emotionally and psychologically I feel smothered—blanketed by lethargy, trapped in a muddy mess of sadness, frustration and anger.

Despite all that I have, I find myself jealous of what others have. I want to be carefree. I want my worries to be about day-to-day crap and not about life or death crap. I want simple decisions to be the focus of my day—like what to make for dinner or what to wear—not decisions about side effects, medications and potentially life-threatening aches and pains.

I'm so frustrated with this confusing dance of treatment and consequences. It seems each step I take towards getting rid of the cancer brings with it a big bag of unwanted complications. Trying to chart the best path requires hours and hours of research, reading and consulting with a host of healthcare professionals of varying specialties.

Right now I'm in the midst of deciding what to do about my breasts—should I move forward with breast reconstruction knowing there is always the possibility of complication, infection or illness? If I do, should I go with the silicone implant recommended by my plastic surgeon even though I've been hearing one too many horror stories about silicone implants being linked to autoimmune disorders and other sicknesses? Should I push to have my other breast removed as a precautionary measure even though my surgeon is not recommending it and the insurance company doesn't want to pay for it? Or just have the other breast reduced and lifted which is a much easier surgery? Does having a double mastectomy improve outcomes with metastatic disease? If the cancer really wants to come back, won't it come back regardless of whether there is a breast there or not?

Last week I made a quick 24-hour trip to NYC to meet with my plastic surgeon where I was joined by my amazing and loving Auntie L who drove down from Massachusetts just to be with me. Thank you Auntie! I expressed my concerns to my plastic surgeon and he reassured me that the decisions were mine to make. He told me I had already gone through the toughest part by having the expander put in. We discussed my options. He answered my questions. In the end, I decided to get a small amount of saline injected into my expander.

The reality is that yes, I want boobs. But I don't want life threatening complications or numerous corrective surgeries. My thinking right now is I might as well move forward with the reconstruction but keep my new breasts very small—in case we need to remove them or the implants—choose saline over silicone implants (for safety reasons), and be prepared to remove the implant immediately if there are concerns.

As I make my way through the new normal that is my life, I keep trying to find healthy ways to deal with the confusion, stress and sadness, ways that don't involve eating rows of cookies or being mean to loved ones. Instead, I'm talking through stuff in therapy, carving out time for walks in nature and meditation sessions, trying to be truly in the moment with Miss M and appreciative of our time together and my time here on earth.

I've been allowing the sadness and feeling the depression. Now I want to pull myself out.

Baby steps. Just gotta take baby steps. One step at a time. Keep moving forward. And trust that eventually I will pull myself out and make it to a better place.

A happy day - grandpa is the special guest for music class

PART 2

*"THE COURAGE TO CHANGE
THE THINGS I CAN..."*

CHAPTER 1

MIXED BAG

OCTOBER 29, 2012

I have to say that things were definitely on the up and up in the days following my last blog entry.

The act of pouring out my feelings on the blog definitely brought on some serious healing—as did the arrival of my in-laws from Brazil, the beautiful summer-like weather and the celebration of my 38th birthday. Even Miss M seemed to be turning a corner and was back to being her silly old self.

The local NBC affiliate aired a segment about me on the nightly news. I was filmed again this past Saturday at a fundraising event for Pink Ribbon Girls, which is this amazing organization in the Dayton/Cincinnati area who provide free meals, house cleaning, childcare and transportation to and from treatment to women battling breast cancer. What a total godsend!

At the fundraiser event I was also lucky enough to meet fellow blogger, Tami Boehmer, and her husband, Mike. Her book, "From Incurable to Incredible" has become like a bible to me. It confirms that you can beat the odds, exceed expectations, be the miracle. Whenever my hope starts to wane, I pick up her book and am reminded that anything is possible.

I also got the good news that my INR blood clotting levels finally stabilized—meaning no more needles in my belly. *Hooray!* I only have to take the blood thinner pills now. Way easier.

Of course, life is never all sunshiny days, rainbows and happy endings...

It turns out that as a result of the Heparin blood thinner shots, my white and red blood count levels have dropped. *Lovely.* I've also packed on close to ten pounds since I started taking blood thinners. According to Internet research, this is a common side effect. *Great.*

And isn't it funny that when I inquired about side effects I was assured there were none. I should have known better. There always is. Oh, the wonderful world of pharmaceuticals.

This got me thinking about how often I end up being the 1-5% that experience horrible side effects from medications. It renewed my interest in pursuing a more natural healing pathway. My oncologist is talking about having my ovaries removed, taking more hormone drugs and continuing with the Herceptin. I'm not so sure I want to do these things.

I know in the end I have to go with what feels right to me. These are my decisions to live with—no one else's. Ultimately, we all want the same thing (I hope)—for me to live as long as possible and enjoy this life.

Still, I'm having lots of anxiety about going against the grain by saying no, refusing my oncologist's suggestions and charting a different path. I plan to meet with a naturopath in the upcoming weeks, as well as another woman who went against the grain and is still here to talk about it decades later. Hopefully, this will help me make some decisions.

This week has definitely shown me what a mixed bag life can be—full of beautiful moments, joy and new adventures—as well as unexpected hiccups and unwanted consequences. I guess the key is to enjoy the heck out of those beautiful moments when you have them and learn to weather the storms. It can't be all good or all bad forever. Somehow, you'll always end up with a mixed bag.

Life goes on. Today I feel good. Tomorrow is a blank canvas.

Here's to hoping we can all pull a few more goodies out of the bag.

CHAPTER 2

YOU GOTTA FOLLOW YOUR HEART

NOVEMBER 4, 2012

Today I was supposed to fly to NYC to see my plastic surgeon, but Hurricane Sandy threw a wrench into those plans. Instead I'm here in Ohio for another week or so.

As I perused through the images of Sandy's destruction I was blown away by the devastation, chaos, lives upended and the sadness and grief. Seeing my beloved city in shambles is tough to swallow. But us New Yorkers are a resilient bunch. The city and its people will persevere. They always do.

Fortunately my family and friends in NYC are all okay. Some are without power (still), some had to walk long distances over bridges from the outer boroughs to get to work, while others rode in cars or trains for three-four hours to get into the city.

And while the Northeast struggles to regain some normalcy, the rest of the country goes on with their lives—myself included. Life goes on.

After a difficult internal struggle, I've made the decision to chart a new path on my cancer journey—a more natural, holistic approach—one that focuses on the power of nature, food, plants, vitamins and herbs, as well as energy work, ancient Chinese medicine and mental/emotional healing. The goal is to nurture the body at its core, restore balance and treat the underlying conditions that led to the cancer in the first place.

It's taken me a while to find the strength to claim this path as my own—saying no to long-term use of pharmaceuticals, going against the grain and the wishes of my oncologist. But I need to follow my heart, my instincts, my gut. I need to make decisions that feel right for me because in the end, it's my life. Although others may be impacted by the decisions I make, I hope everyone can trust I'm making these decisions after much thought and research. Ultimately, we all want the same thing—to keep me alive and healthy for as long as possible.

All week long, as I debated what to do, the Universe kept putting helpful people and events in my path.

First, my Reiki practitioner shared her story. Over a decade ago Renee was told to have a liver transplant or face an inevitable death. She chose to follow her heart and not have the liver transplant and is alive and thriving to this day.

Then the owner of Harmony Farm agreed to meet with me to share her story. She was diagnosed with breast cancer nearly ten years ago. After undergoing a lumpectomy she refused chemo and chose instead to go the natural route—specifically with doctors specializing in anthroposophic medicine (a form of holistic complementary medicine applied by conventionally trained medical doctors). Today she's more than just alive. She's radiant. Her energy is pure health and love. She's an inspiration.

Then two separate people sent me links to movies highlighting the ability of holistic medicine (and specifically a whole-foods, plant-based diet) to balance the body and promote natural healing abilities—*Food Matters* and *Hungry for Change*.

In yesterday's mail I got another movie, *Forks Over Knives,* that speaks again to the power of a whole foods, plant-based diet to heal the body and cure disease. Even Dr. Oz chimed in on this movie saying, "I loved it and I need all of you to see it."

I feel like the Universe is trying to tell me something.

Don't get me wrong, I'm not saying no to ALL pharmaceuticals and Western medicine. If I get a blood clot, I'm taking meds. If the cancer comes back and I need to do more chemo, I will. If my body needs surgery, I'm getting it. I've already done these things once with great success and will do them again if I need to.

But for now, I'd really like to give my body a rest—nurture it, restore its natural healing powers, give it love and let it heal.

This whole thing is also teaching me how important it is to follow your heart. Too many of us make choices based on other people's wishes and not our own, inevitably leading us down a road of discontent and misery.

Why not chart a new path based on what feels right to you? Why not live the life you want to live? Sure, you may ruffle a few feathers in the process, but who cares? Just follow your heart and things will fall into place.

Life is valuable. Don't waste it.

CHAPTER 3

HEALTHY LIVING AIN'T EASY

NOVEMBER 9, 2012

Embarking on my new healthy livin' plan and it ain't easy. Those of you who know me may think, "But she was already pretty healthy." Apparently, I can get even healthier.

Last week I met with a naturopath doctor in Columbus. I found her online and oddly enough, when I called, she told me she was closing her practice here in Ohio because she was moving to—are you ready—NYC. But she did manage to squeeze me in. And fortunately, I'm in NYC a lot these days so we can continue to see each other there.

One of the main reasons I chose this naturopath is because she specializes in women's health issues and seeks to balance hormones naturally rather than with pharmaceuticals. This is big on my list because my breast cancer feeds on excessive estrogen. But I'd rather not take Tamoxifen or Arimedex or any of the other long-term hormone drugs. So balancing my hormone levels has become a serious priority for me.

She is also an expert in botanical medicine, whole foods based supplementation, homeopathy, hydrotherapy and has advanced training in two European systems of medicine— gemmotherapy, which utilizes plant stem cells for their potent healing compounds and biotherapeutic drainage, which facilitates the body's ability to eliminate toxins.

A few days ago I received her long list of recommendations based on our two-hour long consult and have to admit I was initially a wee bit overwhelmed. But piece-by-piece I'm putting it all together.

I understand now why so many people choose to just take a pill. Going the natural route is extremely time consuming, sometimes complicated, costly and a lot of hard work. But for me, it's worth it. I'm healthier and more energetic than a lot of folks I know—despite having Stage 4 breast cancer. And I truly believe this is the answer to keep my cancer from coming back.

The other day I was watching Oprah's interview with Joel Olsteen and he proffered the following statement, "What follows the two simple words, *I Am*, will come looking for you and determines what type of life you will have."

The words hit home with me. How often do we think negative "I am" statements? "I am never going to succeed, I am sick, I am a failure or I am all fucked up (that's a personal favorite of mine)." But how is that gonna help? I believe one of the reasons I'm doing as well as I am is because I continue to believe anything is possible.

Today I choose to say something different. I AM going to beat this cancer. I AM strong. I AM healthy. I AM a fighter. I AM an inspiration.

What are you saying to yourself? Maybe it's time to change your "I am" statement, too.

CHAPTER 4

DON'T DISCOUNT
THE HARD WORK

DECEMBER 7, 2012

This week Miss M and I took off for a weeklong journey to NYC and Massachusetts. I had three doctors' appointments in NYC and fortunately, Auntie L was gracious enough to drive down to keep Miss M happy while I was at the doctor. Although I have to say, keeping Miss M happy in NYC is a fairly easy task—just take a ride on the subway!

People often ask why I chose to have my surgeons in NYC even though I live in Ohio. The answer is multifaceted. Primarily, I chose NYC because it's home, t's familiar and because I'm most comfortable here. I chose the NYC surgical team because they were recommended by a fellow breast cancer warrior and friend. Honestly, I trust the NYC doctors more. They have more experience, impressive backgrounds and amazing skills. Plus, I have a soft spot for my team because they used to work at St. Vincent's Hospital in the Village where Miss M was born.

Of course I also chose NYC because it provides me with the perfect excuse to come back to my beloved Big Apple on a regular basis. Being "forced" to return to NYC every few weeks has been an amazing gift. Spending time there gives me such a boost. It allows me to reconnect with myself and reminds me that there is life outside of suburban Ohio.

This week I received my usual check-in and saline injection from the plastic surgeon, as well as my two-month follow up with my oncology surgeon. Both surgeons said all looks good. I will return to NYC two more times. Then we'll schedule the final surgery for April.

My third appointment this week was a consult with a new oncologist that a friend referred me to. I was looking to get another opinion on what is next for me. The oncologist is a young, charming, smartly-dressed Park Avenue doctor. One of the country's top oncologists, he is charismatic and dedicated to his patients.

He said I was a "complex" case. He wanted more time to review my stack of medical papers before making further recommendations. But he did seem to support the traditional stance that I should be taking meds for the rest of my life. However, when I challenged this by pointing out that my next set of scans will likely reveal no evidence of disease and questioned if it is still necessary to take all these meds when there are no tumors evident, he admitted that's something to consider.

What I took away from the meeting was his recommendation that I stay on Herceptin for the rest of my life—or until my heart can't take it anymore—and that I have my ovaries removed at some point in the near future. He was impressed with the aggressive actions I've been taking thus far and encouraged me to stay on an aggressive path.

What I also took from this meeting was the feeling that I'm being treated like all other Stage 4 breast cancer patients—which I guess is to be expected. Every doctor I see makes similar recommendations. I get the sense they don't think I'll live too long—that it's necessary to endlessly blast my body with pharmaceuticals assuming I won't be around long enough to have side effects.

I consistently feel like all the efforts I'm making to live the healthiest life possible are not recognized by any of the doctors I see, (and) that anything outside of surgery or medication is discounted or "pooh-poohed."

This is where the difficulty lies for me.

I don't see myself the same way. Maybe I'm naive or deluded with wishful thinking but I don't want to go through all this only to have a heart attack as a result of some med I took or die from another form of cancer or organ failure caused by the meds I'm taking.

I'm not done here on this planet, in this body, with this life. I have so much more to give, teach and enjoy. The doctors and their "standard treatment" options can take their death sentences and endless pharmaceuticals and shove 'em. Do not discount my hard work!

I continue to embrace all possibilities and live with hope and faith rather than fear.

Family dinner at one of the many amazing NYC vegan restaurants - with Miss M, Cousin J and Auntie L

CHAPTER 5

GOING AGAINST THE GRAIN

DECEMBER 15, 2012

I recently started taking Herceptin again after a three-month hiatus and the side effects are settling in. These include constant head-aches, back pain, mood changes, hot flashes, exhaustion, cracking skin around my fingertips that renders them utterly useless and painful to the touch (there were a few days recently when I couldn't even type), nose bleeds, dry eyes (no more contact lens wearing), forgetfulness, mental blocks and this horrible sensation of not feeling satisfied by the amount of air I inhale (otherwise known as "air hunger").

It's not even these minor side effects that concern me. Rather it's the long-term damage to my heart that really concerns me.

Now I'm questioning my willingness to continue with Herceptin.

The standard treatment for early stage HER2 positive breast cancer is 52 weeks, which I've almost completed. However, those of us with metastatic disease are often told to stay on Herceptin indefinitely or for as long as our hearts can handle it. But I'm not so sure that's something I'm willing to do.

I just finished watching a disturbing documentary, *Cut Poison Burn*, about the war on cancer and how it's not working. I also read an intriguing book by Shannon Brownlee entitled, "Overtreated: Why Too Much Medicine is Making us Sicker and Poorer."

Both question America's current medical system and treatment methods for common ailments such as cancer. They ask us to consider why death rates from cancer haven't really changed all that much, why more and more people are being diagnosed and why so many people end up dying from the treatment they receive and not the cancer itself. They look at how the pharmaceutical companies, FDA and politicians are caught up in an incestuous relationship that revolves around money instead of truly helping people. Because let's be honest here, cancer is a multi-billion-dollar industry. If cancer patients get better, jobs will be lost and companies will lose a lot of money. It's like the war on drugs. We've been fighting the war on drugs for decades now, but still don't seem to be any closer to achieving a drug free society. Instead, we've been funneling revenue to government agencies and creating a booming prison industrial complex.

It's all about the benjamins, baby.

Don't get me wrong, I'm not saying my doctors don't want me to get better. I'm just saying the system is really, really messed up.

In January I go for my next set of scans. I believe they'll show NED (no evidence of disease)—knock on wood. If that's the case, then in my mind the battle becomes one of prevention rather than active treatment.

It all makes so much sense to me. It feels right to me. The difficult part is convincing everyone else that I'm not crazy for going against the grain and making such "radical" choices. But I'm learning to get over that. I'm listening to my gut, honoring my feelings. And ultimately, these are my decisions to make.

This is my life. I plan on living it to the fullest.

CHAPTER 6

PARENTAL LESSONS ON LIFE

Parenting is one of the most difficult endeavors I've ever taken on. Nothing tests your patience more than an angry, screaming child. Since returning from my most recent trip to NYC Miss M has been a hot angry mess. I'm guessing the timing of these two events is not a coincidence.

Fortunately, we're having great success with Miss M's new social worker. Miss M is opening up more and more each time. She's sharing her anger and fears about mommy's cancer, using little stuffed animals to work through her frustrations, asking questions and expressing her opinions. The sessions are informative and reassuring for me too—I'm receiving confirmation to do what I know is best for Miss M, learning new parenting tools, receiving support in my struggle to be a good parent through cancer and understanding more and more about what's going on in Miss M's precious little head.

The picture of Miss M was taken yesterday. It was "one of those days." Although we had plans to go see the Dayton Ballet perform the Nutcracker, things did not go quite according to plan.

First there was her hysterical fit about putting on her shoes and jacket which led to us being late for the ballet. We were then forced to sit in the "late" seats all the way in the back until intermission when they would allow us to sit in the seats we paid for. Of course Miss M couldn't see from the "late" seats and made her frustration known. That led us out of the theatre where she ended up in a pile on the floor, screaming and crying—much to everyone's horror and amusement. Finally, we decided to just go home.

What I'd hoped and expected to be a beautiful festive family day ended up being a day from hell. And I couldn't seem to shake the bad energy off me. I carried it with me the rest of the day.

Last night, an episode of *Up All Night* finally gave me some perspective. It reminded me days like this do happen and life does not always go according to plan. Finding the humor in these moments is key— laugh, recognize the futility of expectations, remember that we don't have control, take a deep breath, go with the flow and let life unfold.

And always remember that tomorrow is a new day.

Today I consciously made an effort to start fresh. I sipped my morning coffee from my favorite "Serenity" mug—the same one my mom used to drink from each morning. I met Miss M where she was at—a valuable skill I learned in social work school—instead of imposing my own expectations or preferences on her. I paid attention to her. We laughed and played together. And aside from one minor incident over some M&M's this morning, we've had a pretty awesome day so far.

I realize every day offers an opportunity to start fresh, let go of the past, welcome each new moment, do things differently and make better choices.

It's been one year since I was diagnosed with metastatic breast cancer. I'm so grateful to still be here and feeling well, to have the opportunity to celebrate another holiday season with those I love and to live another day.

Wishing everyone a fantastic holiday filled with serenity, beauty, love—and fresh starts.

CHAPTER 7

HORMONAL HEAVEN

DECEMBER 28, 2012

Changes… Changes… Changes…

Yesterday my fabulous Brazilian in-laws finally returned home to Rio de Janeiro after staying with us for two glorious months. We truly loved having them in our home and in our lives. I adore my in-laws.

Today the house feels empty and silent.

It's always a bit rough in the days immediately after our visitors go home—a bit lonely and sad. People often assume it's stressful or taxing for us to have visitors all the time, but the reality is that hubby, Miss M and I love it. We are so lucky to have such loving and caring people in our lives and we cherish the time we get to spend with them.

Now, for the first time in over a year, we have no guests scheduled to stay with us. *How weird.*

Of course, I can never stay put—or alone—for too long. I have another trip planned for next week. This time Miss M and I are head-ing to Toronto (with a quick jaunt to NYC thrown into the mix for my LAST appointment with the plastic surgeon until the spring).

When I return from Toronto it'll be time for my next set of scans—PET scan, echocardiogram and possible CT scan—the results of which will determine my next steps.

At this point my goal is still to get off all pharmaceuticals—for however long I can swing it—because they make me feel like crap.

If my scans come back clean—which I expect them to, a girl's gotta stay positive right?—then I plan to wean myself off the meds and use natural ways to keep my body in balance and the cancer at bay.

I feel especially empowered to do this after meeting with my naturopath today. We reviewed results of the urine and saliva tests I did to measure hormone and adrenal levels and the results are good. I was most excited to hear that my estrogen levels are at a very low and healthy level. They are also in balance with my progesterone and testosterone levels.

This is fantastic news! This means my levels are where they need to be. My estrogen positive cancer does not have any extra estrogen to feed off of. My estrogen has been suppressed without having to take the hormonal meds like Tamoxifen or Arimidex that everyone keeps trying to push on me. It seems you can balance hormones naturally.

My naturopath will continue to monitor my hormone levels in the months to come and together we'll pursue all possible pathways of creating balance—body/mind/spirit—to keep the cancer from coming back.

Choosing to chart my own path is challenging but necessary—necessary for my health, my growth, my new desire to speak my mind instead of doing things based on what other people think and necessary to stay true to myself.

Sometimes you gotta do what's necessary.

CHAPTER 8

LIVING WITH THE INVISIBLE

JANUARY 11, 2013

On my recent travels to Toronto and NYC I was struck by the dichotomy of my two realities. On the outside I'm just another ordinary, healthy looking mom. But the truth, which is invisible to most, is way more complicated.

Breast cancer has changed me. It influences my decisions. It's a nagging voice in my head, a terror that comes alive at random moments. Every little pain is a potentially life-threatening complication, a constant reminder to choose wisely and live fully.

Yet all of this goes largely unnoticed by those on the outside looking in. The battle is invisible.

While it's nice to blend in sometimes it also feels a bit incongruent. There's the *outside* me who appears to be totally fine, and the *inner* me who is waging a war against death.

A part of me wants people to know the truth. I want people to see my scars—to understand how different my life is now and know I am fighting for my life here. I want my struggle to be acknowledged.

It's so weird going about your day-to-day life with these massive internal battles that are invisible to the world around you.

I often walk the streets and wonder who else is living this way. *What internal battles are other people dealing with? Could the barista making my coffee have an abusive husband at home? Is the flight attendant dealing with an autoimmune disorder? Was the girl getting on the school bus raped or molested? Is the garbage man battling depression? Did the clerk at the grocery store just go through a miscarriage?*

All of us have internal wounds and battles, invisible on the outside but felt deeply on the inside. Trying to face our fears, fight our battles and heal our wounds is a lifelong practice.

In my own fight I recognize that the hard work I'm doing is paying off. The effort I make every minute of every day to live a healthier life and heal my wounds is helping tremendously.

But I also live every day with the knowledge that the median survival time for metastatic breast cancer patients is three years—and I've already lived one of those years.

I try not to think about my death. I try to focus on living, on the potential, on the flip side of the coin that tells of women living for decades and on the miracles in life.

Monday I go for my next PET scan. I believe in my heart that the scan will show no evidence of disease. I have to stay in the space of hope.

I've also decided that I'm going to stop taking the Herceptin. My last dose was at the end of December. I haven't told my doctor yet. I'm a little nervous about his reaction. But I'm going to stick to my guns on this one, just as I did with refusing to take the Tamoxifen or Arimidex.

It's a heck of a lot of work to live the way I do, but I do feel great. And everyone keeps telling me I look great too.

For me, there's no other option. I want to live—one day at a time.

CHAPTER 9

JOY TO THE WORLD— I'M CANCER FREE!!

JANUARY 29, 2012

For those of you not on Facebook, we have BIG news today. Apparently I'm now CANCER FREE!

I'm still in a state of shock. Although it's what I willed and wished to happen, it's still a little hard to believe.

This morning I received the results of last week's bone scan and X-rays and indeed they're both clean. *Hallelujah!* We'll continue to monitor the one potentially suspicious spot from the PET scan, which could be something or nothing at all. But Dr. K says I don't have to do another set of scans until sometime this summer.

After leaving the doctor's office I cried big tears of joy. I smiled at the sky, thanked my mom and took some time to go for a walk in the woods and meditate under the trees. The birds serenaded me from above as I tried to wrap my head around the news.

Hubby and I decided to take a family vacation to the warm sunny beaches of Mexico to celebrate. We leave on Monday. I can't wait!

But my journey is not over. I must continue to stay on track with my diet, exercise, supplements, removal of toxins and chemicals and deep psychological and spiritual work. This is my new life. These things are not optional. They're necessary if I want to keep the cancer away.

Meanwhile, I continue to seek beauty in the everyday moments. As my Auntie D sings, "Find the joy in an ordinary day."

One of the little things I really look forward to is my morning cup of organic chai tea. Each teabag has an inspirational message on it. I get such pleasure from reading these.

Today's message was, *We are here to love each other, serve each other, and uplift each other.* How beautiful.

I just want to thank everyone again from the bottom of my heart for your continued support. Thanks to all those who traveled to Ohio to help us; who organized, performed at, donated items, and attended the benefits held in my honor; to everyone who reads this blog and sends me advice and encouragement; and the people who continue to chant, pray and send healing vibes my way. It worked. It really worked. I didn't do this alone. We all did it together.

CHAPTER 10

KEEP ON WALKING

FEBRUARY 13, 2012

The da Silva's have returned from a glorious week in Mexico! We had a heavenly time, spending every day at the beach. We played in the sand, swam with the fish and listened to the intoxicating rhythm of the ocean waves. We mostly did a lot of nothing. It was just what the family needed.

On our last night there I took a walk along the beach after dark. The sky was lit up with stars and I had the whole beach to myself. As I walked I noticed how different the ocean looked at night. It was no longer tranquil and welcoming. The darkness made the water ominous and I felt a bit anxious and afraid. I cut my walk short and returned to our room.

I think so much in life can be terrifying when we're in the dark. I guess that's why we try to plan, control and manipulate things as much as possible—believing this will remove some of the unknown, lessen the fear. In truth, we can plan all we want but life will continue to throw unexpected curve balls. After all I've been through in the last three years I now realize this more than ever.

It also casts my recent scan success in a different light. Yes, I'm overjoyed about the news, but I still recognize the future is unknown—that my scans may not always be clean, the cancer can come back and my journey is far from over.

Miss M tells her therapist she thinks we're keeping secrets from her about my cancer. If I'm cancer free now, she wonders, *Why do I still have so many doctors' appointments?* Although I wish my cancer saga ended with the results of those last scans, that's not the reality.

Today I made calls to start organizing the next piece of my journey. I scheduled my next reconstructive breast surgery, confirmed with my oncologist that it's okay to remove the port in my chest when I go in for surgery and made an appointment with a new holistic cancer team in New York.

The saga continues.

Although the future is still unknown, my journey with cancer has brought me to a better place internally. I'm a different person now—more grounded, present, easygoing, less controlling, better able to deal with life's difficulties and fully aware of my blessings and the beauty of my life.

I continually seek to acknowledge the dark places, fear and the unknown—but then I keep on walking forward, refusing to let fear hold me back from exploring all that is in front of me.

CHAPTER 11

SO NOW WHAT?

MARCH 6, 2012

*S*o *now what?* I find myself asking that question a lot lately.

I'm feeling better, so now what? I've gotten rid of the cancer, so now what? All major crises are temporarily diverted, so now what?

Even though I'm in the midst of figuring out logistics for my next surgery and my treatment is technically not complete, I feel different— like I'm ready to step into my new life, start the next chapter.

I recently joined forces with some local social workers to help them birth a promising new non-profit and signed up for Marie Forleo's B-School with the hopes of gaining some clarity about my career. I'm also entertaining the thought of writing professionally and using therapy sessions to explore my passions.

I've found there are many ways to respond to life's horrors. I've tried quite a few over the years—from deep denial and numbing myself with drugs after being raped at age 21 to pushing down my feelings and running on pure fumes after my mom died in 2010. But this time I decided to try something new. I elected to face the horror head on— feel the terror and still go on with life, take the difficult steps necessary to transform myself from within and actively try each day to use the horror as a lesson on living.

For all of you out there facing your own personal horrors, you can make it through.

Ask for help. Search within. Love yourself. Face your demons. Make peace with the struggle. Seek to discover why the horror has come to you. Ask, "So now what?" Then use the journey as a starting point for a new way of living.

CHAPTER 12

HERE WE GO AGAIN

MARCH 16, 2013

Another major medical procedure is drawing near and Miss M is starting to freak out.

She's become a little leech, stuck to me, unwilling to let go. I can't go to the bathroom, leave the room, take a shower or make a phone call. Her tantrums are out of control—anger, fear, sadness, worry—it's all there in her precious little three-year-old self.

I don't blame her one bit. It's hard enough processing everything as a 38-year-old with some life experience, let alone as a fresh-faced preschooler. This is hard on everyone. I get it. Cancer sucks. And we're all a little angry, fearful, sad and worried.

It's so damn hard dealing with her out of control behavior and not knowing what to do about it. The other day we were stuck on the side of the road for 45 minutes while she just screamed, yelled and cried and refused to get in her car seat. Of course I can't physically gain control in these situations because every move she makes has me immediately shielding my chest, scared she's going to break my breast expander or dislodge my medi-port. So what do I do? I just sit there. I sit there and listen to her scream, cry, wail, whimper and spit up all over herself. And I wait for it to end because I don't know what else to do.

I realize these extreme moments mostly happen when she's tired or hungry. Plus, right now we're transitioning into the "no more naps" stage, which I'm sure isn't helping matters—nor did the recent time change.

I also know she's pissed that I'm going to NYC without her on Monday. When I told her she immediately asked if she was going too and looked heartbroken when I told her she wasn't. How do I explain to her that it costs a lot of money to keep flying us both out? That I don't want her to keep missing school? That sometimes it's easier to go to my appointments without her?

What's a mom to do?

I know her feelings are very close to the surface. She's trying to process what's going on and what's about to happen. On the flip side, she just started telling me over and over again, throughout the day, that she loves me. "Mamãe, I love you," over and over, at random moments. It's so damn adorable. I love her too. So, so much.

Thank God for therapy—hers and mine. Miss M's therapist is amazing. Apparently Miss M spoke about her worries I was going to die and her fears about the pain I might have in surgery. The two of them are brainstorming ways Miss M can help me after surgery—bringing me water, lying down and reading books with me and giving me hugs and kisses. And they talk about ways for her to vent her frustrations— by hitting her pillow or stomping her feet.

Thank god she's talking about this stuff with someone.

I swear being a parent is by far the most difficult thing I've had to face in this life. (Well, okay, facing breast cancer is up there on the list too). I remember my mom always telling me I was her biggest teacher. I get it now. I understand, mom.

That's all I can do—try my best to understand and then remember oftentimes there is no answer. No understanding why. It just is what it is, nothing more—and you gotta just deal with it.

You can't control the hand that you're dealt, but you can choose how to play it. Sometimes if you play your cards right, you can even win the game with a really shitty hand.

CHAPTER 13

MAKING PEACE WITH THE UNKNOWN

APRIL 1, 2013

When you are in tune with the unknown, the known is peaceful— quote from my chai tea this morning.

This has been one of the bigger lessons on my cancer journey, accepting the unknown and releasing the urge to control. In doing so, I've come to a greater sense of peace—both with the unknown and the known.

I know I have surgery in nine days. The plane tickets are booked and the housing arranged. My support team is lined up—hubby is taking off work to be by my side, my Massachusetts team is taking over on "mom" duty and grandpa is flying from Bowen Island to help out post-surgery. I know my surgeon plans to remove my chemo port while he's in there. I know today is the first day I've been without blood thinners since October—which is thrilling and terrifying at the same time.

I also recognize that all of these seemingly "known" pieces of my life can change in a flash.

Instead of stressing or worrying about the surgery I'm just staying focused on today and focused on this week. Miss M is beyond excited. Our daily countdown to Friday's departure elicits a loud "yippee" and a megawatt smile each time we talk about it.

Lately Miss M is talking more about her concerns about the surgery, her hatred of the cancer and her fear about me dying. I'm just so happy she's sharing this stuff with me. I know it helps that I'm talking to her about everything much more openly now, too.

Our new morning ritual is to answer a question from the fantastic, "3-year journal of Q&A for kids," that Cousin J from Astoria sent us. Each day Miss M and I eat breakfast and ponder our answers to that day's question.

Yesterday's question was, *What do you try to forget about but can't?*

Miss M's answer: "I don't want to remember your cancer."

A few days ago, during one of our kitchen dance parties Miss M started singing her own tune—and I quote, "Go away cancer... We don't like you cancer... We fight you cancer." She belted it out at the top of her lungs to some make-believe tune she made up while we shook our booties all around the kitchen. It was priceless.

Yes, she's still clingy. Yes, she still has tantrums. Yes, she still drives me crazy. And yes, I still worry about her—but less and less so lately. I'm putting into practice a lot of the parenting advice everyone's offered—I'm sticking to my guns, not letting guilt fuel me, trying not to baby Miss M or solve all her problems, talking openly about what's going on and taking her to therapy. So far it seems to be working. Thanks to each and every one of you for your suggestions. I'm listening and it's working.

I finally feel that life is heading in a positive direction—for the first time in a really, really long time.

At Friday's appointment with my oncologist he actually used the word "REMISSION." He called me his "miracle patient." Damn that feels good!

While I know there are no guarantees, I'm much more in tune with the unknown these days. It makes dealing with the everyday dramas and "knowns" of life—like surgery—so much easier.

CHAPTER 14

MY NEW NORMAL

APRIL 9, 2013

Miss M meditating at our favorite beach, Round Hill

My heart is fluttering. My heart is aching.

I'm sitting on the Amtrak train heading to NYC, towards my next surgery. Heading away from my family, friends and my darling Miss M. *Sigh...* I miss her already.

Miss M and I had a fabulous weekend in Massachusetts, spending time with those we love—play dates, sleepovers, nature walks, chitchat, lots of hugs and laughter and some much-needed time by the ocean.

Yesterday she and I spent two hours at the beach just playing, running around, collecting sea glass and shells and meditating on the ocean waves. I shed a few tears thinking about my mom, feeling her presence around me. I also felt a profound, intuitive knowing that everything was going to be okay—the surgery, the recovery, the aftermath. It was the same knowing I felt on the beaches of Long Island in the weeks after my initial diagnosis back in 2011.

I'm learning to live with this disease, to accept my new normal. I'm getting better at navigating the ups and downs, at finding the balance between the two worlds I live in—the "normal" world and the metastatic cancer world.

When people ask if I plan on maintaining my new complicated way of living for the rest of my life, the answer is always "yes." It's my new normal, my medicine. I'd much rather live this new complicated life than be forever popping pills and IV'ing pharmaceuticals.

This is the balancing act I face for the rest of my life—one foot in the normal world and one foot out. I go through my days like anyone else, yet forever hearing the reminder deep inside me that I have a terminal illness. Lurking, stalking, ready to pounce and take over at a moment's notice. Forever knowing I must remain vigilant in my fight—carrying containers of supplements everywhere I go, struggling to find restaurants where I can eat, wondering if each ache and pain is something more serious, anticipating the results of scans and blood work.

Yet all that being said, I truly feel cancer has brought me to a better place. I like the new person I'm becoming. I feel more at peace, grateful and more in love with life than I have in a long time. While I'd never call cancer a gift, I can see the gifts cancer has brought me.

It's funny how when you're able to see the gifts and lessons contained in life's toughest moments, the world suddenly expands and your place in it becomes rich with possibility.

Here's to life's possibilities, uncovering gifts and finding balance in an uncertain world

CHAPTER 15

SURGERY UPDATE

APRIL 13, 2013

I survived yet another surgery. Hopefully, it'll be my last.

By all accounts the surgery went well. I went in to the OR around 10:00 am on Wednesday and woke up again around 3:00 pm. Upon waking, I wasn't puking all over myself like last time (thank god!) but was still nauseous for a good 24 hours. The entire team at Beth Israel Cancer Center was friendly, helpful and competent. Although I haven't looked at my breasts yet, hubby has and he says they did a really good job. *Yay!*

The pain has been relatively minor. Today, so far, I've managed with no meds at all.

They've got me wrapped up in a surgical bra I wear day and night until the swelling goes down. There was a bit of encapsulation on my left breast—where the skin & muscle tissue had hardened around the expander—so there was a bit more "digging" on that side to get the expander out and my implant in. I also ended up with a drain on the left side which got clogged yesterday and required a quick visit with my surgeon. But all is well today.

Generally everything seems easier and less painful this time around. I'm still feeling weak, tired, groggy and dizzy a lot but I know that will fade with time. Tomorrow hubby and I check out of Hope Lodge in Manhattan and head to Long Island to stay with family. Miss M will also be arriving tomorrow with Auntie L. *Hooray!* Hubby and I are missing our little girl like crazy. I've got a follow-up appointment with the surgeon on Thursday and then we're scheduled to fly back to Ohio next weekend.

Until then we plan on relaxing, enjoying our time together, getting out in the sunshine, taking some train rides with Miss M and toodling around NYC.

I'm still so happy with my decision to do surgery in NYC—to have such an amazing surgical team in the comforts of my favorite city, close to family. I wouldn't have done it any other way.

Thanks to everyone for your continued prayers, support, love and assistance. I'm so blessed to have such an amazing community of family and friends all over the world who have truly been there throughout this cancer journey. I love you all—and will forever be grateful.

CHAPTER 16

FAMILY LOVE

APRIL 21, 2013

The da Silva's have finally returned "home" to Ohio. As always, it's bittersweet.

Miss M is overjoyed to be back with all her stuffed animal friends, hubby is thrilled to be sleeping on his comfy king size bed and I'm happy to be back in my kitchen, reunited with my juicer. But it's always difficult leaving the northeast, our families, friends and the cities we love to return to the homogeneous heartland of the mid-west.

I saw my surgeon on Thursday for post-surgery follow-up. The drain was removed and I can't do any vigorous exercise for another four weeks or so. I must wear my itchy surgical bra 24 hours/day for the next four weeks (yes, I even have to sleep in the damn thing) and I can't drive for another week or so.

It's been eleven days since the surgery and I'm feeling pretty good— my mind is clearing; my body continues to detox from the anesthesia, surgery and pain meds; and I started my new 30+ pills a day vitamin and supplement regime. The pain has been minimal—so minimal that it tricks me into thinking I can go about my normal activities—until I do. And then the pain starts.

Hubby has been absolutely amazing today, helping with everything, anticipating what needs to be done, playing with Miss M, doing laundry (folding too!) and preparing the extra bedroom for my dad's arrival. I joked with him, "Who are you? What happened to my husband? And can I keep you instead?"

I took my second real shower today since the surgery and finally had a good look at my new breasts. *What a trip.*

For most of my adult life I've had droopy DD cups (except when I was pregnant, gained 50 pounds and went up to a 36F!). Now all of a sudden, I have small perky breasts. Even though my right breast is still real, after being lifted and reduced it's so damn perky it looks fake to me. I have no idea what the end result will be but I'm guessing I'll have a nice set of 34B cups. For the first time since I was twelve, I may actually be able to go bra-less—which opens up a whole new world of clothing options (hello, lil' strappy sundress!).

Big shout-outs to my family—both in Massachusetts and NYC—for making this surgical experience so seamless and stress-free. Once again, my gratitude cup runneth over. And I'm reminded of the importance of community, family, letting go and not trying to go it alone.

CHAPTER 17

TERRI GOT HER GROOVE BACK

MAY 16, 2013

Spring is officially here (well at least in Ohio, it is)! My surgery is done, I have no more treatments scheduled or drugs to take, I got myself a new pixie haircut and am starting to feel like I'm getting my groove back. *Hallelujah!*

I saw Dr. K this week. He agreed that my NYC surgical team did a great job. Dr. K asked if I'd gotten my period again and I was thrilled to tell him, "Yes!" (I've only had three visits from "Aunt Flo" since I was diagnosed in November 2011). To me, getting my period again is a signal that my body is finally starting to re-balance itself, detoxing the chemo and other meds, getting back to normal.

Of course in the estrogen positive breast cancer world, getting your period is something you don't want. Dr. K said as much, encouraging me to consider options like surgery and more meds to permanently put my ovaries out of commission and end my periods once and for all. I nodded politely, murmured a few "I knows" under my breath, but thought secretly in my head, *No way!*

No way am I going back to menopause land at age 38. No way am I going back to a world where sex is painful and devoid of pleasure. No way am I giving up this recent upsurge in my sex drive that actually has me wanting sex with my husband for the first time in almost two years. No way am I going back to hot flashes, brain fog, night sweats and sleep problems. *Screw that!* Nobody talks about the sexual side effects of cancer, but we so need to.

Luckily Dr. K is open to the work I'm doing with my naturopath to naturally lower and re-balance my estrogen levels. Although Western medicine takes the approach that estrogen is bad and we need to remove it all from the body to prevent cancer from happening, the reality is it is much more complex than that. This is probably why most conventional doctors don't address the issue in a more in-depth manner. Instead, most offer the standard response. Take Tamoxifen and suppress activity in your ovaries—either through surgery or more meds—period.

As long as my estrogen levels remain at healthy levels and my body continues to have no evidence of disease I'll continue to keep taking action the natural way.

Besides, I'm loving the fact that I've got my groove back after going for such a long time wondering if it would ever return (and I think hubby is loving it, too)!

Life is pretty good these days. Having my dad here has been great for both Miss M and me. She follows grandpa around all day. She can't wait to wake him up in the morning and requests he be the one to read her bedtime stories. She sits as close as possible to him at the dinner table, in the car and everywhere else. The two of them are a great pair—chatting away with each other, listening to each other's goofy theories and stories and just being silly. It's adorable. And it's giving me a much-needed break to write, rest and have a few moments to myself.

On Monday the party gets even better with the arrival of our beloved Auntie Cole who's coming for a weeklong visit. *Hooray!*

So far, the recovery from this surgery has been a hell of a lot easier than the last one—for everyone involved. I'm determined to make this surgery my last. Although I'm not in denial about the realities of metastatic disease, I refuse to live through a lens of fear.

Life is tough. Shit happens. Challenges are inevitable. But I, for one, am determined to let go of suffering and fear and stay in the groove instead.

CHAPTER 18

ENJOY IT THE BEST YOU CAN

MAY 24, 2013

L iving with metastatic breast cancer is such an odd reality. You're caught in a place between life and death and aware your days may be numbered

Facing your own mortality changes you.

I'm supremely aware of the passing of time. I don't want to waste precious moments in the day. If I didn't have to sleep, I wouldn't. I just want to make the best use of each moment. I see the gift of life and I plan to enjoy it as best as I can.

I'm headed back to NYC in two weeks for my final follow up appointment. What a trip just writing that. After ten months of biweekly visits back and forth my surgery appointments will finally be done. Plus, Dr. K says he doesn't need to see me until sometime this summer after my next set of scans. My blood no longer needs to be checked on the regular. I'm a free woman!

Mind you, I'm a free woman who's also fully aware this freedom may not last forever. So again, I plan to enjoy it the best I can.

The night before Mother's Day, I had a dream where my mom came to me. It was my mom during one of the happiest periods of her life—young, healthy, at the height of her dance career. She opened her arms wide and I just went in and hugged her and hugged her. It was so comforting and beautiful and full of pure love. It was the best Mother's Day present ever.

Days later, my therapist and I were discussing the dream and she asked me to retell it, but this time as my mother. Almost instantly I am in tears. As my mom, I tell myself that I'm surrounded by love—not just from her, but from so many others—all my family and friends that have passed on and all those that are still here. And I feel it. I feel the love. And it's beautiful. And I know it will help carry me through. I know it's the love and blessings that have helped to get me to this point; helped me heal, cope, reclaim my life and reclaim myself.

I'm in the midst of reading Lissa Rankin's new book, "Mind Over Medicine: Scientific Proof That You Can Heal Yourself." For the last few months her name continued to pop up in front of me, so I ordered her book and I'm loving it. Her message of addressing physical illness through a holistic, multifaceted lens that considers mind, body, soul and environment is exactly how I've been tackling my cancer diagnosis.

My first appointment last night with my new functional nutritionist was also amazing. There was a 45-minute intake session that explored everything from my mom's pregnancy and the circumstances surrounding my inception, to how I handle stress and of course my medical history. They're going to review my blood work, supplements and current eating habits to create a customized food plan that will optimize my health, boost my immune system, balance my hormones, detox my body and keep the cancer at bay.

I know living this way isn't for everyone. It takes a lot of time and energy and a big commitment. But I have to say it's worth it. I've never felt better.

I'm committed to living my best life possible and enjoying it the best I can.

CHAPTER 19

A REPRIEVE FROM CANCER WORLD

JUNE 8, 2013

Miss M, grandpa and I just spent a week in Massachusetts visiting with my mom's family. We went up to Provincetown to visit my mom's ashes on May 30th for the third anniversary of her passing. I can hardly believe it's been three years already.

The event was a full-on family affair—three cars, nine people and many hours spent loving, sharing, shopping and eating. And of course many tears shed as well.

Now grandpa, Miss M and I are in NYC going to doctor's appointments and hanging with my dad's family. Being here immediately puts me at ease.

It's been two months since my reconstructive surgery and I continue to be surprised and delighted in the fact that everything turned out so well. My surgeons all agreed my breasts and I were looking good. I got the go-ahead to start exercising again, lift more than five pounds and stop wearing bras.

Dr. B (whom I love) was genuinely happy to see how well I was doing. She seemed surprised I wasn't on any meds and curious about what I was doing. We talked about diet, supplements and living healthy. I told her about my choice to switch over to a more natural and holistic treatment path and shared my disappointment that things like diet, exercise, supplements, emotional support and mental health weren't discussed more with patients. Dr. B told me it isn't necessarily that doctors don't recognize the importance of these things. It's just they don't want to overwhelm patients, especially in the beginning— which I totally get.

I do see the cancer world opening up more and more to complementary approaches, which is awesome. Recently there's been talk about new drugs that treat cancer by triggering the immune system. The immunotherapy drugs have shown promising results and offer fewer and less toxic side effects.

While I'm all for less toxic drugs, it begs the question, why not boost your immune system naturally without drugs? Start exercising. Eat healthy. Meditate. De-stress. Take a few supplements. Have more fun. All this will boost your immune system, too. Personally, I'd much rather do it that way. Oh, but wait—there's no money in that, is there?

It's funny how treating my body like a temple instead of blasting it with complicated pharmaceuticals and excessive scans and toxic treatment makes me a radical.

While in Massachusetts, my nearly 85-year-old grandmother ranted to the TV about the cancer industrial complex and how they'll never find a cure for cancer because then they wouldn't make any more money. Hearing the words come out of her mouth was surprising, beautiful and hilarious all at once. It also made me realize just where my own feisty "radical" ways came from.

Right now, I'm so thrilled my life is not all about cancer—for a little while at least. I've moved from monthly and weekly visits to the semi-annual appointments. This means more time to just live, enjoy the people I love, tackle things on the bucket list, dare to live fully, embrace every opportunity and figure out the next chapter.

Having cancer has definitely changed me. It got me back in touch with my intuition, inner wisdom and soul. It challenged me to transform my world.

The beauty is that contained within the pain and suffering of life, there's always the possibility for growth and transformation.

CHAPTER 20

BIG NEWS/BIG CHANGES

JUNE 21, 2013

There's so much going on. Where do I even begin?

Let's start with the good news. Hubby got a new job! And it's in Connecticut! After two years in Ohio we're finally moving back east—to the ocean, the family and the hustle and bustle of the northeast. We'll be settling down half-way between the families in NYC and Massachusetts. It's perfect—close, but not too close. And it's happening right now! Hubby starts his new job on July 1st.

We're in the midst of move prep which is always fun (not). We're trying to figure out what town to move to, whether to rent or buy, cancelling services, organizing our lives, etc. We should be old pros at this by now. In the eleven years hubby and I have been together we've moved eight times. This will make sweet number nine. Hopefully it's the last move for a very, very long time.

The three of us plan to leave tomorrow to start our two-day road trip to Connecticut to find a place to live and get hubby settled. We also have a family wedding on the Cape next weekend and the fabulous Auntie Cole is going to be in NYC, so Miss M and I have a little trip to the Big Apple on the calendar as well.

There's lots of stuff going on—including the not so fun stuff—like the fact that I got another blood clot. This time in my left arm. Luckily it's not high enough on my arm that they had to check me into the hospital with IV blood thinners. Instead, I had a brief stint in the ER, an ultrasound, a few visits to my oncologist, some prescription meds and I'm back on the blood thinners. Because we're traveling for the next week or two, I have to give myself the damn heparin needles again until I'm back in Ohio and we can regulate my Coumadin dose. I'm not thrilled at all about doing the shots in my belly—especially when hubby's not around and I'll actually have to administer the shot myself for the first time. But I'm thrilled we caught it early.

So the million-dollar question is why did the clot happen?

It's been ten weeks since my surgery. With many of the risk factors gone, I began to ask, *What is my body trying to tell me? What's the lesson?*

Ever since my second surgery I've been stressing and living in fear of getting another blood clot, obsessing about it. A part of me thinks my body got tired of living in a state of perpetual fear and just said, *"Fine, you want something to be scared about? Here, have the damn blood clot and let's be done with it."*

Then I went to my trusted Louise L. Hay's book, "Heal Your Body." When I looked up blood clots this is what was written: *Closing down the flow of joy. Lack of joy. Lack of circulation of ideas.*

Reading those words hit me at my core. This is exactly what I've been feeling lately— actually, more than just lately. For the longest time I've put my dreams on hold for other people.

As a side note, this is what Louise Hay writes about the underlying causes of breast problems: *A refusal to nourish the self. Putting everyone else first.*

So me! Pretty wild, huh?

I really think this blood clot is just a reminder of more lessons I need to learn, a manifestation of my own lack of joy and my over-thinking and worrying about getting another blood clot.

I need to just let the fear go, recognize the lessons, move forward and stop looking behind me.

It's definitely a time of change. I feel the next chapter is going to be a good one. A really good one. Fingers crossed.

CHAPTER 21

DOING THINGS DIFFERENTLY

JULY 3, 2013

What a whirlwind! Life has been pretty intense lately with all the traveling, staying in different places and prepping for our upcoming move. It's a lot.

My body was definitely telling me to slow down and take better care of myself. My face broke out, my back ached, my head hurt, I had no energy and was an emotional wreck—not good.

Cancer loves broken down, stressed out bodies. I wasn't eating healthy or exercising. There was no time for meditation or supplements (which were temporarily put on hold while my naturopath adjusted dosages because of the blood thinners). I was exhausted and under a whole hell of a lotta stress—not good at all.

But now I'm back in NYC. I've handed over the reins on the house hunting to hubby and I'm enjoying a few days with the fabulous Auntie Cole before heading back to Ohio with Miss M to pack up our lives.

I remember my therapist asking me, "When life gets stressful again, what will you do differently?" Because it's not a matter of "if" life gets stressful, it's "when" life gets stressful. And the last time my life got super stressful, I didn't know what to do.

Last week, amidst all the stress, I resorted to many of my old unhealthy patterns. But then my therapist's voice rang in my ears.

So mid-week I finally got my ass into the gym at the hotel and squeezed in some exercise. I tried to eat healthier. I loaded my body with green juice, smoothies and veggies. I found time to just relax and enjoy nature, be with family, de-stress and celebrate life.

And I'm feeling a lot better.

The last week and a half brought me back to so many of the lessons I know I'm here to learn. It reminded me of how my unique self and the circumstances of my life are not coincidence. We're here for a reason. Each one of our lives has meaning and purpose. Staying open to the lessons in our particular journeys and responding with courage to honor our true selves brings us closer to living the life we are meant to live.

For me, the lessons are a matter of life or death. And I'm not looking to die anytime soon, so I gotta keep learning, growing, striving, flexing those muscles and keep believing that anything is possible. It is, right?

CHAPTER 22

BIDDING FAREWELL TO OHIO

JULY 20, 2013

The time has come to say goodbye. Miss M and I officially leave Ohio this Friday. *Wow.*

The days are now full of goodbye hugs, tears and promises to stay in touch. I'm saying goodbye to the cornfields, farms, wide-open sky and to lots of fantastic people who made living here more enjoyable than I ever imagined it could be. I'm saying goodbye to my therapist and just today my soul sister and Reiki healer, Renee. Monday is my last evening with the girlfriends and Miss M and I are now going through the house, recalling favorite memories from each room. Today we remembered our dance parties in the kitchen and birthdays in the backyard.

Don't get me wrong. I'm THRILLED to be moving. There's a lot about life in Ohio that I will not miss at all—small town mid-western living just ain't my style. And for that, I am psyched and oh so ready to be starting our next chapter in Connecticut.

Our new life is slowly starting to take shape—we're in the midst of closing on a beautiful little home only a mile from the beach, hubby is loving his new job, I found a great Montessori school for Miss M and

I'm finally getting clear about what I want to do professionally. It's a beautiful thing.

The last few weeks have been pretty insane, though. With hubby already in Connecticut, I'm stuck with all the move stuff while still acting as a full-time—temporarily single—mom. Luckily Miss M has been pretty great lately, playing by herself, helping me clean the house and going to bed without too much drama. It's awesome because a month ago she was totally insane! I'm not sure if it was the therapy sessions she started going to again, her picking up on the joy and excitement hubby and I have about this move or just that she's getting older. Who knows? I'm just thankful every day she is my daughter. And I tell her that, too—how she is just what I always dreamed my daughter would be.

With everything that's been going on, it's been hard not to fall back into old patterns. I'm finding the most important things I can do to stay balanced are to ask for help and make time for myself. The old me would have done neither of these things. The new me, however, is finding time amidst the chaos to exercise, go to Reiki, laugh with friends and enjoy the sunset. The new me gets babysitters, hires cleaners and asks people for favors. This manifestation of self-love is such an integral piece of healing and living your best life.

Speaking of which, I'm finally reading Bernie Siegel's book, "Love, Medicine & Miracles." It is totally amazing and brings me back to my fascination with the mental and emotional roots of cancer.

Society tells us not to look at the roots or causes of disease. Disease is what it is. You're sick—take a med, have surgery. But to me the roots of illness are so important. I don't really believe illness is random. We get sick because something is wrong in our lives, off balance. Illness is a wake-up a call, a call to get honest, get real, look around you and figure out what's not working—and change it.

Even though I'm ready to start the next chapter in my life, I know I'll never fully close the chapter on cancer. No matter where I go, metastatic breast cancer follows. It is a constant reminder that tomorrow is never promised.

So I continue to live for today, love myself, be kind and remain open to the game changers of life. Goodbye, Ohio. Hello, Connecticut!

CHAPTER 23

I VOW TO HONOR MY TRUTH

AUGUST 3, 2013

We made it to Connecticut. *Hooray!*

Miss M and I are settling into our temporary home at the hotel with hubby. It's not so bad living in a hotel—free breakfast, swimming pool, maid service. But I'm itching to get into our actual home with our belongings organized and all my kitchen stuff at my fingertips. It looks like it'll be a couple more weeks before that happens.

In the meantime Miss M and I are spending our days with family and friends, having fun at the beach, planning trips to Sesame Place and Provincetown, celebrating birthdays and exploring our new neck of the woods. I have to say our new neck of the woods is pretty fantastic—ocean beaches, seaside towns, acupuncture clinics and health-food stores. I'm loving it.

But as I start my search for a new oncologist I'm really missing my old one—Dr. K. He was such a gift— open minded, encouraging, humble and kind—a truly great man and doctor. It's going to be hard to find someone as amazing as him, but I'll look far and wide to find the right doctor to continue this journey with me.

Finding the right doctor is a serious issue. They become a part of our lives. How we feel about them and how we feel when we're with them is integral to our health on every level.

This week I had an appointment with potential oncologist #1. Unfortunately, the visit didn't go so well—at least not for me. I left the appointment with doubt and fear coursing through my veins, chipping away at my confidence and hope. I began questioning everything: *Am I naive to think I can be the 1-2% who show no evidence of disease for the rest of my life? What if something does show up on one of my scans? Am I willing to do more chemo or Herceptin or drug treatment? Am I digging my head in the sand because I don't like to dwell on the fact that most metastatic patients, like me, are in treatment for the rest of their lives?*

After some tears, family hugs and a few glasses of wine, I'm pushing the fear away and trying to step back into a place of hope, faith and positivity. You know what? Fuck the haters! Fuck the doubters!

Look, I know the stats. I know the odds aren't in my favor. But doesn't that give me even more reason to take a chance? To experiment? To go against the grain? What have I got to lose? Either way I could be dead in two years.

I'm realizing again and again how difficult it is to be a patient who charts their own course. I need a team that respects my decisions and recognizes that I'm not choosing my path blindly.

Regardless, I vow to not let the haters get me down—I will surround myself with positive and helpful healing allies, honor my intuition and make choices based on what feels right to me, live my life to its fullest and be a force for good in this world. That's the way my mom did it and I respect her for that—big time.

I will keep repeating my mantra with each breath I take—*Healing energy in... Cancer and fear out...*

CHAPTER 24

A DOSE OF REALITY

AUGUST 14, 2013

The latest news on the cancer front is that my tumor markers have risen. Bummer, I know. But I'm not gonna freak out. I'm just using it as a catalyst to get myself back on track.

The CA 27-29 is a blood test that monitors tumor markers in breast cancer patients. It's far from foolproof and not commonly used as a guaranteed predictor of anything. Many doctors use it as an additional tool to monitor disease progression or possible return. I usually get tested every four-to-six weeks. Normal is below 40 and I have been consistently between 30-40 for a while now. Until a few weeks ago. Now it's 70. *Ugh!*

As I said, I'm not freaking out. I know things like inflammation (hello recent surgery) and stress (hello recent move) can cause a temporary rise in tumor marker levels. I don't doubt that with everything that's been going on lately, my body just went on overdrive and produced a few more cancer cells. I also believe that as my life settles down and I get serious about living healthy again, my levels will go back to normal.

Knowing this I'm working hard to assemble my new healthcare team. Not only do I need a new oncologist, I also need a Reiki therapist, physical therapist, psychotherapist and a naturopath. So far, I think I've lined up two out of the five. Fingers crossed that my upcoming appointments work out and the new Graceful Woman Warrior team will be complete.

A few nights ago I had my first Reiki appointment here in Connecticut and it was awesome. I went in with pain, tension and stress and left feeling relaxed and rejuvenated. I told her nothing about my recent surgery or the pain I was in. Despite that, she instinctively knew what parts of my body needed healing.

I don't know if Reiki works because I believe it will or because there is a genuine energetic shift inside me during our sessions. I know the mind is powerful. I also believe that the world, and all living creatures, are simply energy. We're able to shift and be shaped through energetic pathways that are beyond scientific study. Not everything can be explained, rationalized or understood. There's definitely something bigger out there, beyond what our human brains can comprehend. And for whatever reason, Reiki and I just seem to work well together.

I always say everything happens for a reason. The way I see it, the rise in tumor markers was an example of what can happen when I get stressed and off track—a dose of reality. Yes, you have advanced breast cancer. Yes, it can kill you. Yes, you need to take this seriously. Yes, you need to get your ass back on track.

This morning I explored the forest hiking trails that are within walking distance of our new house. A few minutes in, I discovered a majestic babbling creek shaded by gorgeous oak trees and I was immediately crying tears of joy. During my Reiki session this week, I imagined a healing place just like this—with big leafy trees and sunlight peeking through the branches above. Now it was here in front of me. I looked to the sky, tears streaming down my face and said a big thank you to my mom and the Universe for bringing this to me—just moments from my new home.

Today, despite all the unsettling aspects of my life, I'm still filled with gratitude. I'm thankful for the beauty and healing energies of nature, the gift of our new home, these gorgeous seaside towns, the support and love that continues to surround us, this next chapter in our lives and for the gift of another day.

CHAPTER 25

THE UPS AND DOWNS OF LIFE

SEPTEMBER 2, 2013

It's been an insane couple of weeks—ups and downs, pain and joy, a little bit of everything. I guess that's life, eh?

On a high note, I am absolutely LOVING our new home. We're slowly settling in, finally unpacking the last few boxes, making this house our home and getting to know the neighbors (who are lovely). We've been bicycling down to the beach and loving the oceanside weather.

People thought I was crazy to let hubby put an offer in on this house, sight unseen. But I know my man. I know he understands what's important to Miss M and me. And he knocked the ball right outta the park. This little seaside home is truly our little piece of heaven.

On a slightly lower note, I've been in some serious pain the last few weeks—from a dull ache in my left arm, through some major cricks in my neck, pains in my shoulder and breast and lots of swelling.

Luckily, I had two doctors' appointments last week. The first was with my plastic surgeon in NYC who said I looked fantastic and the swelling was likely related to the blood clot and not the surgery or overexertion. We measured my arms, confirmed the swelling and agreed I needed to speak with an oncologist.

Three days later, I met with potential oncologist #2, Dr. H. With oncologist #1 being such a disaster, I was praying this one would be better. Thank god she was.

Dr. H respected my choices and my time. She had read my file before our appointment and agreed with my plastic surgeon that it was probably an unresolved blood clot in my arm causing all the drama. She told me Coumadin doesn't work with all cancer patients and switched me to a new injectable blood thinner, Arixtra. It's been three days since I started the new meds and I swear the swelling, redness and pain is getting better. *Hallelujah!*

But I'm still thinking, *What the hell is this blood clot situation all about? Why does it keep coming back? What is blocking my flow?*

I'm trying to dig deep and figure out the answers—find my flow and open up to joy.

For starters, I'm tackling items on my bucket list and getting back to my social work roots. I signed up for piano lessons and next week I start a training course with the Prison Mindfulness Institute. They bring meditation and mindfulness practices—including yoga—to local prisons in order to help prisoners grow, transform and heal. It's not a full-time social work job, but it's a start. I'm also joining Bernie Siegel's famed Exceptional Cancer Patient (ECAP) support group, which I'm over-the-moon excited about. There's lots of good things on the horizon.

But the recent health issues took hubby and me back down the path of fear, realizing how quickly things can take a turn for the worse—including the possibility of chemo again, or even death. We were reminded of how important it is to prioritize self-care.

We agreed I need to take a little time-out from all my traveling to just stay put for a while and batten down the hatches. We need to get settled in to our new life here and get back into a routine—which means, unfortunately, I have to cancel trips to NYC and a long over-due trip to Bowen. *Sigh...*

The other thing I continue to do is analyze my dreams. I believe our dreams are a window to our soul and subconscious. My dreams this week all involved difficult or horrible situations I was able to over-come—getting my car unstuck from the sand, rebuilding a brand-new kitchen in a burned down house and successfully kicking out home invaders. My subconscious seems to be telling me this is one crazy dif-ficult road to go down. But it won't kill me—not yet anyway.

It ain't gonna be easy. But I'm up for the challenge.

CHAPTER 26

SCAN RESULTS AND
MESSAGES FROM ABOVE

SEPTEMBER 13, 2013

First, I have to say thank you for all the amazing comments after the last blog. *Wow!* All that support, encouragement, love and vulnerability had me laughing out loud and wistfully pondering big questions about life.

All the love couldn't have come at a better time.

On Wednesday I got the results of my most recent set of scans. It wasn't what I had hoped for, but it wasn't nearly as bad as it could be.

The good news is the ultrasound of my arm showed no more deep vein blood clots (which is awesome) but there's still some circulation problems—restricted flow and superficial clots in peripheral arteries.

The not so good news is my tumor marker level is up again (from 35 to 70 to 90 now). The PET scan shows the cancer is trying to set up shop in my body again. There are clusters of cancer cells spreading from my thyroid area, through my chest, and into my left armpit. Most of the spots are pretty low on the SUV scale and may still be associated with inflammation from the surgery and stress of the move. A few seem pretty serious and may be partly to blame for the circulatory issues and pain I'm having on my left side.

I'm trying not to freak out but the first day was hard. I shed some tears. I even thought about just giving up for a moment. Then I thought, *Enough with that. Let's look at the positive— the cancer hasn't spread anywhere beyond the immediate chest area which is great news. There were a few suspicious spots in my leg but they didn't light up on the scan so I'm not wasting my energy thinking about them. My energy is still good and I'm still living life.*

Still, my body is definitely not happy. The pain is nearly constant. Luckily, it's just a dull ache—nothing deep or sharp, but still totally annoying. My poor body is screaming out to me to make changes, to get back on track.

So I'm going back to the basics—re-reading Kris Carr's, "Crazy, Sexy, Diet"; trying hard to get my eight hours of sleep each night; assembling a kick-ass healthcare team; making time for meditation, visualization and affirmations; doing my daily exercise and drinking my green juice and smoothies.

What else can I do? Well, my oncologist offered me what Western oncology has to offer—meds—period. Either more chemo meds or more anti-hormonal meds or meds to stop my ovulation. No, thank you—at least not for now. When I go inside and ask myself what feels right, it's not taking more meds.

I have a new naturopath on my team who is awesome and brilliant. She and I are meeting next week to come up with a plan of action. I'll keep my oncologist up-to-date and then we scan again in another three-to-four months and take it from there.

Yesterday morning I went for a run through the woods and ended with a meditation on the beach. I looked to the sky and asked my mom for help. I cried and I tried to visualize the waves washing through me and carrying the cancer away. I breathed in the salty air and tried to shift my energy.

Later that day, Miss M and I were cleaning the house when I saw a little red fox pass by the window. I knew it was my mom talking to me, sending me a message of hope and support. When I looked up the symbolism behind the fox it said foxes bring energy of magic, increased awareness and opportunity. The fox reminds us to enjoy life and have fun. The fox is a trickster and reminds us to be adaptable and curious. And just the night before my cup of chamomile tea held the message *be curious* on its tea bag. *Hhhmmm...* The Universe—and my mom—are definitely trying to send me a message.

I'm going to remain curious and aware, keep thinking outside the box, trust my intuition and stay open to the magic and messages that appear around us every day.

CHAPTER 27

TALKING TO MYSELF

SEPTEMBER 23, 2013

A weird thing happened at the beach the other day. It seems I made peace with the idea of death. I was at the beach meditating and suddenly got the message that death wasn't something to be afraid of—I had to just surrender, let go of all the stuff I can't control (hello serenity prayer) and make peace with the idea I will die at some point. We all will.

In the next breath I thought, *No, wait! I can't be okay with death. Won't that signal to my body that I'm ready to go? I don't want to die. Not yet.*

The more I reflect on the experience, the more I realize letting go of fear and accepting death is a good thing and an important piece of being able to surrender. Trusting and knowing everything is a part of the master plan—each challenge, every person we encounter, all our experiences—everything happens for a reason and the goal of it all is to lead us to living our highest purpose and being our most authentic selves.

One practice that brings me closer to living this way is meditation. I'm also doing daily affirmations and visualizations. When I was doing chemo, I visualized dancing ladies like the Rockettes going through my body and kicking my cancer cells apart and out of my body. Now when I'm meditating at the beach, I imagine the ocean waves washing through me and removing the pain and cancer cells.

I've also gotten into the habit of asking myself questions out loud and waiting for an answer (yes, talking to myself!)—like the day I was in pain during the hour long "rest period" before going for a PET scan. The pain in my arm wouldn't go away so I asked it, *Pain, what do you want? What is the lesson here?* And I heard back, *Humility.* Alrighty... Yesterday, I asked the pain in my neck, the cancer, what it needed. And I heard the answer, *Love.* Okay. It's interesting what comes up when you allow yourself to just sit and be silent.

I met with my new naturopath, Dr. J, on Friday. She's a professor here in Connecticut who just wrote a textbook on Naturopathic Integrative Oncology. She knows her stuff. She's also Cherokee Indian and a deeply spiritual person. It was hubby who found her from a simple Google search. *Go figure.* Now she's helping me formulate a multi-step holistic healing plan which involves mental and spiritual work, diet changes, supplement revisions, herbal remedies, nightly castor oil applications, hormone balancing and regular acupuncture to help with the pain.

Dr. J was the one to tell me the good news that my tumor marker number actually went down. Yes, you read that right. It went down instead of up on the most recent test. *Oh yeah!* A small decrease, but a decrease nonetheless. I'll take it.

In other news, I was recently contacted by Katie Ussin of Channel 2 News in Dayton. Last year she did a piece on me for her weeklong breast cancer awareness tribute. This year she wanted to do a follow-up with all the women she interviewed, including me (via Facetime on my phone).

Also on the calendar next month is my friend and colleague, Eryka Peskin's program, "31 Days & 31 Ways to Jumpstart Your Abundance!" For each day during the month of October, she's going to share tips, tools, and exercises that cover all the areas needed to live a more abundant life (health, money, sensuality, love, work, mindset and more). And I'm one of the guest contributors.

All-in-all I'm feeling pretty good these days. I'm still trying to figure out how to handle my ever changing "normal"—how to deal with the fact that my body is not what it used to be. Some days are fabulous. Others, not so much.

Last night while reading the story of another cancer warrior Leah Putnam, on her site, "Wholy Cancer," I was reminded that cancer is not some foreign object inside me. It's a part of me, created by me. It's my own cells—only mutated. So I can love it because loving it means loving myself. Healing it means healing myself.

In the meantime, I'll keep talking to myself and asking the big questions.

CHAPTER 28

NOT LETTING FEAR
GET IN THE WAY

OCTOBER 10, 2013

I've been struggling lately, caught up in the fear—the fear of my cancer being back and the fear that this inspires in everyone around me.

I'm finding it really hard not to allow other people's fears to invade my thoughts and take root in my body, especially as I choose to treat my body the natural holistic way. The idea of that scares people. Makes them uncomfortable.

I'm realizing it's not about them and what makes them uncomfortable. It's about me—my life, my decisions. And yes, it's scary sometimes—going out on a limb, doing things differently, refusing the usual standard of care. But maybe all the encounters with fear and doubt from others is just a test. How strong is my faith? My belief? Am I willing to honor my truth? Trust my intuition?

Last week I reached out to my mom, the heavens and the Universe for guidance. Since then a number of perfectly placed healing paths have presented themselves to me.

First is my newfound love of running, something I never thought I was capable of (I was the girl who couldn't run around the field in elementary school without getting cramps). Lately I've been running the streets, the trails and the parks with ease. The beautiful part is that when I'm running, the daily pain miraculously disappears. I become entirely focused in the moment. The "runners' high" takes over and life feels good, so I keep doing it.

Another thing that sustains me is my ECAP support group with Bernie Siegel. I had my third group this week and was so inspired, touched and boosted up by the energy of everyone there. We're different ages with different cancers, different treatment plans and different stories but we all share a common outlook of hope and possibility.

At the end of group, Bernie always does a guided meditation. This week he had us envision our current self and our "ideal" self, taking a trip together. Where are we going? What is our ideal self like? Well, my ideal self, Lola, and I were going to Venice—getting lost in the alleys, eating delicious food, drinking wine and laughing out loud. When I asked Lola what I needed to do to be more like her, she said, *Have fun!*

Bernie then asked us to merge our two selves and the tears were streaming down my face. When I opened my eyes the other facilitator leaned over and told me, "Just find your joy, honey. Do things that bring you joy!" It was as if she read my mind. That group is amazing.

To top off my week, I managed to find the most amazing acupuncturist. After going to two sessions this week, it's definitely working. I'm beyond thrilled at the new insights, reassurance, support and oh yeah—pain relief.

So I keep doing the work—including signing up for a two-day meditation retreat in December, looking for a sangha to practice with, finding a new therapist, re-doing my vision board, working through

Lissa Rankin's amazing and thought provoking "prescription for health" from her book, "Mind Over Medicine," and even trying to squeeze in a 15-day writing to heal challenge with Michelle Pammenter Young (a fellow breast cancer warrior in British Columbia).

Although I still feel like so much of my life is about cancer, at least when I focus on nourishing my soul and spirit I don't feel the resentment that usually crops up when I focus strictly on my physical self.

Maybe it's time we all thought about what life we want to be living, who our "ideal" self is and how we go about getting there. I still believe anything is possible.

CHAPTER 29

RECLAIMING MY LIFE

OCTOBER 23, 2013

The time has come. I'm on a quest to find myself and reclaim my life.

I took a major step towards this goal last week—I bought myself a round-trip ticket to Europe to go on a spiritual healing pilgrimage. *Hell yeah!* I'm SO EXCITED! In less than two months I'll be heading to Portugal, France and Italy for an eight-day solo journey to three different healing sites—Fatima, Lourdes and San Giovanni Rotondo (to get me some more Padre Pio healing oil). I'm taking a few days in Venice, too. I'm going in with no expectations, no attachments—just wonder, joy and curiosity.

Booking these tickets was such a huge step for me—being away from my precious four-year-old, stepping away from my role as mom, wife, daughter, household manager and cancer patient. Until last week taking an international trip by myself seemed like an impossible dream. My "roles" in life have come to define me and take on some weird supernatural importance. Then I realized my roles had become more important than my own life, interests, passions and dreams. *How did that happen? When did this happen?*

I'm in the midst of reading Anita Mooriani's book, "Dying To Be Me," where she recounts her near-death experience from cancer and how the experience brought her back to life and ultimately healed her. It's an amazing and thought-provoking book. Her reminders about unconditional love, seeing the world through fresh eyes and living your truth reinforce my own beliefs and reconnect me to some of the fundamental tenets of living fully and without fear. The book also reminds me of the power of the mind, the possibility of miracles and the importance of connecting with spirit. I'm sure it's no coincidence that I'm reading this now as I struggle to reclaim my life and embark on my own spiritual journey.

I realize things have to change. I know I'm on the brink of something utterly fabulous. I just need to keep putting one foot in front of the other until I get there.

So I will.

I will travel, dance, read and write. I will laugh, spend more time with my favorite people just like I did last weekend at our housewarming party and live for myself and not just for others. I will try new things and have more fun!

And I will keep putting one foot in front of the other and trust that eventually, I'll reach that utterly fabulous place that I know is just around the corner.

Or could it be that I've already reached it?

CHAPTER 30

DECISIONS, DECISIONS, DECISIONS

NOVEMBER 1, 2013

It's been a wild week with a housewarming party, Auntie Cole's visit, a quick bop up to Massachusetts, a trip to my beloved NYC and a ton of appointments—I definitely got off track. When I returned from NYC a few days ago I was inflamed, tired and in pain. The sight of me triggered some intense fear in hubby.

We had a serious discussion with him pushing me to do chemo or take meds and me totally confused about what to do. I understand that ultimately we all want the same outcome—for me to be alive and well. The problem is that we just can't agree on the best way to achieve that outcome. I want to do this naturally. Everyone else wants me to go the Western medicine route.

Unfortunately, cancer is a very tricky and complex disease. There's no one size fits all treatment plan that will work for everyone. Despite all the advances in medicine the death rate from cancer is virtually unchanged since 1950. Some live while others die. There are no guarantees.

I know I have major decisions to make. I recognize the severity of my diagnosis. My decisions are not made lightly or uninformed. There's plenty of research that supports the choices I'm making. Even if there wasn't, the choice is ultimately mine to make.

I'm very thankful for the few people that do support me—my naturopath who gives me the 411 on how we are directly attacking certain cancer cells with supplements and herbs; my fabulous holistic nutritionist who continually fine-tunes my diet by maximizing cancer fighting foods and working within the parameters of my meds and food sensitivities; and then there's my amazing acupuncturist who is constantly enlightening me about the meridians in our body and the spiritual side of my cancer.

As far as I'm concerned my plan is working. I went for an ultrasound this week and the results confirmed no more blood clots. *Hooray!* I'm continuing to wean myself off the Arixtra blood thinner with my oncologist while my naturopath re-introduces more blood thinning supplements. The ultrasound also confirmed the swelling in my chest and arm was inflammation, just as I suspected. My blood flow is constricted because my veins are pretty small and the tumors are pushing on them.

My acupuncturist has been documenting the size of my tumors as we go through treatment and one has decreased in size by half already. This week I'll be getting another blood test to check my tumor markers. Fingers crossed they're still relatively low as well.

One of the big lessons I learned over the last week is that if I plan to actively treat and heal myself naturally I really need to give this 110%. There's no pussyfooting around. I have to get hardcore.

Some of you may question how it's even possible to get more hardcore than I already am. Oh, it's totally possible. Hubby challenged me to think about whether I'm really capable and willing to get that hard-core. After thinking about it for 24 hours I decided I can and I will.

Yesterday I had a great talk with Chris from Chrisbeatcancer. com. He beat colon cancer without chemo ten years ago and has a great website that showcases stories of natural healing and what he's learned along the way. He spoke about the four main causes of cancer aside from genetics which only accounts for a small number of cancers— diet, lifestyle choices, environmental pollutants and stress. He advised me to get stricter with the diet, adding in lots more juicing and a diet of primarily raw fruits and veggies, cutting out ALL added sugar and processed foods, saying "no" to certain people and activities and giving myself the space to truly focus on healing.

I'll continue on this path and give it my all until my next set of scans in December when I return from my spiritual pilgrimage in Europe and decide what's next at that point.

In the meantime, I continue to search for the lessons in life—to remain open to my healing journey in whatever form it takes and make a promise to myself not to make decisions from a place of fear.

PART 3

*"AND THE WISDOM TO KNOW
THE DIFFERENCE..."*

CHAPTER 1

RETURNING TO CHEMOLAND

NOVEMBER 14, 2013

I've been sucked into a vortex—a seemingly endless space of sadness, self-pity and pain. It's no fun living in this space. I've been here before. I don't want to be here again. Yet I can't seem to pull myself out. Out of the endless crying and depression. I feel I've lost my spark—my fight, my mojo, my inner warrior.

Sigh...

Three days ago I made the decision to move forward with more chemo. I start today.

I'm not thrilled about the decision but feel it's necessary at this point. In the last three weeks the pain has gotten out of control. My tumor markers rose from 90 to 245. The circulation is practically cut off in my shoulder and arm. Most mornings a few of my fingers are numb. When I went to put up Miss M's hair in a ponytail for ballet class the other day, I couldn't twist the elastic with my left hand. My entire left arm is swollen—cancer swollen. The swollen that reminds me of my mom's body when the cancer took over and she was spiraling toward death. I need help. Hopefully chemo will be the help I'm looking for.

So off we go again to chemoland...

I had a new port surgically inserted into my chest by a wonderful radiologist who did her medical training at NYU (instant brownie points). As they wheeled me into the operating room I felt the love, support and prayers of everyone surrounding me. It brought tears to my eyes. I was awake for the whole procedure—which I actually preferred—and the pain has been manageable.

Yesterday I went in for an echocardiogram to make sure my heart is strong enough to handle treatment.

This morning I meet with my oncologist. I'm set to do two of the three drugs I took the first time around (almost two years ago)— Taxotere and Herceptin. I'll be taking the medications through my port once a week. We haven't discussed end dates yet. Right now I'm just trying to get the tumor load reduced before December so I can take my trip to Europe without being in pain.

Let me tell you, being in pain completely sucks. After living with chronic pain for the last three months I can sympathize with those suffering from painful chronic illnesses like fibromyalgia and arthritis. *My lord!* The pain just wears you down. How can you enjoy anything when your body is constantly screaming at you? I just want to tell it, "Shut the fuck up! Leave me alone! Let me enjoy my walk in the woods, my meditation, my family dinner!"

While I know it's well and good to feel our feelings, I also know staying stuck in them is not healthy. I know that negativity, stress, fear and depression compromise my immune system and feed the cancer. I can't get stuck in this. I've been here before, I've pulled myself out before and I will do it again.

I watched a couple of clips from Oprah's Super Soul Sunday with Kris Carr and Mark Nepo and their experiences with cancer. I realize

I need a lot more of this—to surround myself with lessons, wisdom, gratitude, acceptance and spirit. I feel most alive when I'm learning, growing, or connecting with other spiritual folks. This is integral to who I am.

I know I need to make life about living again and not just about avoiding death. As Kris Carr said, "I may never be healthy on paper, but I can still be healed, healthy and whole at my core."

Hopefully, this chemo will kick my cancer back to the curb. I know I'm the only one stopping myself from achieving my dreams and truly living life for me—not for hubby, Miss M or the cancer—for me. It's time I get out of my own way, put the excuses aside, step out into the fear of the unknown and truly live life.

CHAPTER 2

HANGING IN THERE

NOVEMBER 19, 2013

I t's been five days since my first chemo treatment and I'm hanging in there. It hasn't been easy though.

First night post-chemo I awoke at 3:00 am with severe pain that nothing could touch. I waited it out, watched some TV and went on with my day trying to survive on 4-5 hours of sleep. The next night I popped a Percocet and with hubby's help watching Miss M, managed to sleep for over twelve hours, which my body desperately needed.

Physically, the pain has ebbed and flowed through all hours of the day. My left is arm is still totally swollen and the sensation from my shoulder to fingertips is mediocre at best. Everyday tasks like typing and washing dishes are becoming more and more awkward. It seems I can never fully get comfortable. There's always a part of my neck, shoulder, breast or arm tugging on my awareness, expressing discomfort.

Mentally, I've also struggled since Thursday's chemo session. Not so much with my decision to do the chemo—which I'm feeling pretty at peace about—but more with trying to swallow and accept my new reality.

My family lovingly took Miss M for the weekend to Massachusetts to frolic, have fun and take her mind off of her messed-up mamma. While I normally relish the alone time, this weekend I found not having Miss M around left me simmering in self-pity and sadness with nothing outside of "me" to focus on. I struggled to get through the day. I ruminated on the unfairness of it all. Maybe I needed to go there? But I didn't want to stay there.

I read and re-read all the beautiful, loving and encouraging thoughts shared on the blog, via text or email, and it helped me make it through the toughest moments. Your words make me smile, help connect me to my strength, reassure me and restore my faith.

I think a big piece of my internal struggle is about fully accepting my life—accepting the unknown, accepting there's only so much I can control. Despite knowing the reality of most metastatic breast cancer patients, I believed I would go through my initial treatment, be cancer free and stay cancer free—period, the end. I'm not sure I ever fully accepted the reality that I will live with this for the rest of my life. Even if I am in remission, cancer is still lurking in the shadows so I can't be "done with it."

Yesterday I woke with a conviction to be done with the pity party. I met the day with a clean slate. I made myself a cup of delicious organic coffee (life's too short not to drink coffee anymore) plus my usual 30-ounce glass of green juice. I took the dog out for a walk by the ocean and stopped at a bench along the way to meditate and express gratitude for all that is good in my life. Even though I still can't get a sports bra on to start running again, I pushed myself to do a modified jog down the block and back holding the dog leash in one hand and my one jiggly breast in the other. What a sight!

I also had a great talk with my naturopath who didn't berate me at all for starting chemo. Instead, she cheered me on and offered supplements to help ease the side effects of treatment. Over the weekend my old oncologist, the fabulous Dr. K, phoned me from Ohio. I had faxed over my recent test results to get his opinion. He spent 20 minutes on the phone giving me the biggest pep talk ever. I was in tears. Finally, for the last two minutes he actually spoke about my treatment plan and agreed the chemo regime should work just fine. He said there's no reason to expect that I won't have a complete response again. He gave me his cell phone number and told me to call any time—god bless his soul.

With all this cheering, support and love how can I possibly give up?

I'm trying to harness all the positive energy and strength I can find. I'm making lists of things I can do to boost my soul and pull me out of the pity party madness, spending time with uplifting people, reading practical books (I am in the midst of re-reading, "The Happiness Project," and loving it just as much the second time around), taking walks in nature, spending time by the ocean, contemplating the big questions and dreaming about the future. I'm also seizing any and all opportunities (like the chance to see Anita Mooriani this weekend in NYC!), doing research about my upcoming spiritual pilgrimage to Portugal and Italy (can hardly believe I leave in less than three weeks) and of course, through it all, remembering everything I have to be grateful for.

I will meet this challenge head on. I have faith in myself and the Universe. I trust that each piece of our lives, each moment, is part of the master plan. This cancer will not take me down. Not yet.

CHAPTER 3

QUESTIONING MY BELIEFS

NOVEMBER 27, 2013

I'm sitting here in the chemo chair as the drugs drip into my body—questioning life, questioning my beliefs, questioning it all.

Life is real confusing these days. Each day brings new questions, fresh insights and a tumble of emotions. I spend my days perpetually on the verge of tears, feel hyper sensitive to people's moods and I'm simultaneously trying to heal the past, envision the future and remain in the present. I know I'm over thinking things and yet I can't stop. I know what I need to do and yet it's so hard to just do it. It's all starting to take a toll on me—the chemo, surgery, pain, exhaustion, frustration, emotions, the chemo brain. *Aaaahhhh!*

We did another ultrasound to check my arm for blood clots because it keeps swelling to ridiculous proportions and nobody can tell me for sure what's causing it. It turns out the veins and blood flow are fine—no clots. That's good. My oncologist figures the swelling is because of the tumors clogging up the lymph system and preventing it from doing what it needs to do—a lymphadema of sorts. We'll consider a sleeve for my arm (sexy) and some physical therapy. The hope is that the chemo will knock those tumors down and free my lymph system to start functioning properly again.

On this day before Thanksgiving I'm really trying to hold onto the moments of gratitude and trying to remember all that I have to be thankful for. But I'm just tired—mentally, physically and emotionally. My body is not happy. My body is not well. And it's hard to move past it.

But all is not lost...

Even though I was tired I went to my Bernie Siegel support group last night. I needed it. On the way home I had time to reflect—to take in the wisdom of my fellow group members, absorb the uplifting support and ponder what I'm doing with my life. As Bernie says, "It's not about avoiding death. It's about living life!"

Last weekend I had the privilege of going to a symposium at the New York Open Center on near death experiences with Anita Moorjani and Eben Alexander. It was a magical event that was made even more magical because my half-sister came along. Each speaker had amazing insights about the meaning of life and what happens after we die. I found myself in tears numerous times throughout the day. I think the main lessons I took away were the importance of living from a place of love and not fear, making self-love a priority and to make the choice each moment to seek out joy and surrender—to surrender control, surrender trying to be something you're not and surrender to what is.

Lately I feel like I'm all talk and no action. I know what I need to do but I'm not doing it. So tomorrow, on Thanksgiving Day, I vow to take action and live from a place of gratitude, love and surrender. Then I'll try to do it again the next day. And the next day. Until one day, I'll look up and realize how much fun I'm having living life and not avoiding death anymore.

CHAPTER 4

WATCH OUT EUROPE-
HERE I COME!

DECEMBER 8, 2013

It's official—I'm going to Europe! *Woohoo!*

I got the green light from my oncologist but didn't make the final decision until I got into the chemo chair for treatment #4 and happened to sit beside a lovely lady named Vivian. It turns out Vivian's family just happens to be from the town of San Giovonni Rotundo in Italy where Padre Pio's shrine is. Padre Pio is the reason for my whole trip—to get more of his healing oil. Vivian's family personally knew Padre Pio and used to regularly bring fruit from their trees to keep the friars nourished. The moment I heard Vivian's story I knew it was the Universe telling me to take this trip. *Do it now. Don't wait.* So I'm going. I leave tomorrow. And I'm over-the-moon thrilled!

My itinerary includes a few days in Lisbon, a visit to Our Lady of Fatima, a stopover in Rome, some serious time with Padre Pio in San Giovanni Rotundo and a final pit stop in Venice. The challenge will be to honor my body, rest when I need to and go with the flow instead of pushing myself to see and do it all.

On another positive note, I think I'm finally starting to feel better. I'm pulling myself out of the depressive funk, I'm back to exercising again (low key walks instead of running), and my confidence and inner strength seem to be returning. It helps that the pain has been more manageable.

Plus grandpa has arrived and he'll be here for the next six weeks! *Hooray!* Having my dad here is a gift. Just watching the joy in Miss M's face as they play rhyming games and tell each other stories totally warms my heart. Miss M loves her grandpa. I couldn't go on this trip without his help. Thanks dad!

All of this is good news despite the fact that my tumor markers don't seem to be getting much better. We're four weeks into chemo and already talking about changing up the drugs or adding new ones. My oncologist and I specifically talked about Perjeta (aka pertuzumab) and Lapatinib. I've gotta do more research before I decide. Plus, I had an MRI this week and the results came back with two tiny suspicious spots on my prefrontal cortex that are not confirmed to be cancer but definitely something to keep our eyes on.

There's much to think about—thank god I have an eight-day solo spiritual journey ahead of me to contemplate what's next.

I realized last night just how much I've been operating from a place of fear lately. I guess it's hard not to when your body provides a painful reminder each day of your own mortality. And it's even harder still when those around you are drowning in fear and leaking their fearful energy all over you. But it has to stop. I have to surrender this fear and give it to god.

On Friday I met with my fantastic naturopath (and was accompanied by Auntie L who loved her just as much as I do). She's thrilled for my upcoming trip to Europe. At the end of our session she reminded me to stay open on my journey—to be aware and fully present to all that is around me. I'm asking the Universe for guidance so I better be ready to receive it and recognize that the answers and lessons may appear in unexpected packages. Watch out Europe, here I come!

CHAPTER 5

REFELCTIONS FROM EUROPE

DECEMBER 17, 2013

My spiritual journey through Europe was just what the doctor ordered. I'm leaving with a renewed sense of strength, an increased sense of inner peace, a quieter mind and a lot less fear. I'm many steps closer to surrendering control and trusting the Universe.

The journey has also opened me up to the Christian faith. Most of my life I've had an aversion to the word "God." My parents were raised in Catholic families, went to Catholic schools and attended mass regularly (heck, my dad even entered the seminary for a brief period in his teens). But they grew into adults who openly detested the Catholic Church. As their child, their dislike somehow became a part of me. Even though my mom was an extremely spiritual person—even an ordained Soto Zen Buddhist monk—the word "God" was never used in our house and organized Christianity was shunned. I was never baptized. We never went to church. Our spirituality involved walking in the forest or sitting by the ocean in silence.

On this trip I found myself admiring the conviction of the faithful Catholic folks around me, their deep sense of devotion and their ability to trust in God and surrender. Now I find myself using the word

"God" for the first time in my life and being okay with it. I also feel compelled to find a church when I get back home.

The healing energy I felt at Fatima, Padre Pio's church, and the grotto of Saint Michael the Archangel was undeniable. I spent hours in prayer and meditation—on my knees shedding endless tears, asking for guidance, releasing my sadness, fear, worries and attachments, basking in the silence and soaking up the beautiful energy of unconditional love.

While a part of me had hoped for spontaneous healing, a miracle of some sort, an apparition or divine intervention, it hasn't happened—yet. But I did experience many smaller acts of God.

Just this morning I was waiting for the 9:00 am bus from San Giovanni Rotundo to Foggia where I was scheduled to catch the 10:30 am train to Milan, and the bus driver told me the next bus wasn't until 1:00 pm because today is a special holiday and the buses run on a different schedule. *Oh okay, I'm screwed.*

Before I had time to get stressed a young lady started talking to me (luckily, she spoke some English). Before I knew it she was calling her brother to come pick us up and drive us into Foggia. *Thank you, Universe!* I made my train with time to spare! I tried to slip them some cash but they wouldn't take it. Turns out her father is in Padre Pio's hospital in a coma. She, her brother and mother all take turns traveling to visit him. I told her about my cancer and spiritual pilgrimage and we promised to pray for each other. What a beautiful gift.

My whole trip was like that—full of gifts, kindness and beauty.

One of the biggest gifts was the lack of pain I've had this week. Aside from the first day I arrived in Lisbon when I was seriously jet-lagged, I haven't had to take any pain meds—none. This, despite the fact that the cancer doesn't seem to be shrinking any, the hair on my head is falling out by the fistful and the swelling in my arm is still pretty bad. This, despite the fact I've totally ditched my healthy diet and had plenty of pasta, sweets and wine. Also very interesting, is that any pain or discomfort I did have disappeared entirely when I was at a religious site praying or meditating.

As I prepare to head home I hope to continue to nurture my new-found sense of spirit and faith. That's always the real challenge, right? Maintaining serenity back in the "real world."

I have some serious decisions to make about my treatment. One thing I do know is that I'll be requesting a biopsy when I get back. I had a dream the cancer is different this time, so I want to get it tested.

In the meantime I'm excited to go home—to hold my daughter and listen to her sweet voice, cuddle and make out with my husband and to eat a great big salad.

As I set off on this journey I thought, *Who does this? Going on a solo international trip to four cities in two different countries in the middle of chemo treatment?* Oh yeah, that would be me! By doing this, I have reclaimed a piece of who I am—the nonconformist, the warrior, the adventure seeker.

I am still a Graceful Woman Warrior!

Outside the Belem castle in Lisbon

CHAPTER 6

TURNING POINTS AND MORE REFLECTIONS FROM EUROPE

JANUARY 7, 2014

Happy New Year!

It's a new year and time for a fresh start. I love fresh starts. I try to remember that each day offers a chance at a new beginning, each moment a turning point towards something better.

Hubby and I have been on a spiritual quest since I returned from Europe—searching for a spiritual community that blends nicely with my Buddhist background and hubby's Catholic upbringing. We're hitting up all the local churches—Baptist, Catholic, Episcopal, United—you name it. And we're bringing Miss M along for the ride. I can already see that she understands the sacredness of meditation, prayer and being in church. I feel like we're connecting more as a family since we started our church exploring, too.

I continue to draw on the strength and serenity of my spiritual journey to Europe. I feel like my whole life shifted since I took that trip—my depression lifted, my decisions are no longer based in fear, I'm enjoying life more, speaking my mind, surrendering and feeling more hopeful.

I remember the thrill and joy I felt as I flew into Lisbon—the tears would not stop coming, so I just let them fall as I watched the sun rise over Portugal from my little airplane window. And the tears continued throughout my time there. Being in Portugal felt comforting and uplifting—it felt like home, which makes sense when you consider my heritage and connections to both Portugal and Brazil. I devoured meals of seafood and fresh olives, walked the magical winding streets of the Alfama District, listened to live fado music and took the tram to see the Monastery of Jerónimos and the Belém Tower (and was delighted that the trams run on an honor system with no one keeping track of who pays). That's the kind of place Lisbon is—friendly, beautiful, charming and trusting. I fell in love.

When I went to Fatima my heart grew even more. In this small Portuguese town Mary appeared to three shepherd children numerous times over the course of a six-month period, culminating in a "miracle of the sun" that over 70,000 people reportedly witnessed. I had heard from a friend just how awe-inspiring Fatima was but still wasn't prepared for the level of magic, energy and healing that would overcome me as I set foot in the Chapel of Apparitions where Mary reportedly appeared. Immediately I was overcome with emotion. I was on my knees crying and sobbing, snot running down my face, puddles of tears pooling by my knees on the floor. It was as if I felt all of humankind's suffering at the same time, while I felt the radiant and unconditional love of Mary and all "mothers."

My pain disappeared. My thoughts ceased. Even though I was only partially sheltered from the outside I was not cold. I stayed there for hours, praying, meditating and crying. Each time I thought I was done crying, I was surprised by another burst of fresh tears. I prayed for those closest to me, for those caught in the struggle of cancer and illness and for all of us dealing with life's difficulties and traumas. I lit candles and said more prayers. I didn't want to leave. But eventually I had to.

Since that day my pain has all but disappeared. The swelling in my arm continues to go down. The tumors in my neck and shoulder appear to be getting "softer" and smaller. My headaches are gone. My energy is returning. My attitude has completely shifted. All of this has happened despite the fact that my tumor marker numbers are not getting better and the strength and dexterity of my left arm and hand has deteriorated to the point where I can't even scrape leftovers from a frying pan.

This Thursday I'm scheduled to start a new drug— Perjeta. My oncologist is hoping it will add an extra kick to the Taxotere and Herceptin. When I asked how long she suggests I continue with chemo her response was basically for as long as I can tolerate it. As of right now I seem to be tolerating it very well. My white blood counts haven't dropped. My red blood counts are a little low but nothing to worry about. My immune system has stayed pretty strong and I credit all the holistic treatments I'm doing for keeping me healthy.

For now I'm choosing to focus on the fact that I'm pain free and feeling good. The fact that I can still function, be an active mom and live my life is what matters. I'm choosing not to focus on the tumor marker numbers or the things that I can't do, or the fact that my fingers are cracking open, my nails are falling off, my hair is gone and my libido is shot.

With the New Year upon us, I'm actively seeking to identify my non-negotiables and make them a priority. For me, this includes daily prayer and meditation, regular exercise or movement, healthy eating, finding time to read and write, traveling, quality time with my family and connecting with people (those I already know and those I've yet to meet).

Here's to a fabulous 2014 for everyone. Let today be the turning point that leads you to discover and prioritize your own non-negotiables of life. Each day, each moment, offers the opportunity to make a choice. Are your daily choices in line with what you value and deem most important?

My new haircut

CHAPTER 7

YES, THIS IS REALLY A NEW POST—WITH SOME FINAL REFLECTIONS ON EUROPE

JANUARY 23, 2014

It seems my email subscribers have been receiving old posts masquerading as new posts in their in-boxes. Sorry about that. To clarify—no, I'm not in Ohio, nor did I have recent surgery. I'm still here in Connecticut, still doing chemo, still soldiering on.

As the old posts came in, I thought it would be neat to re-read them myself, to revisit life as I went through treatment the first time around—two long years ago. Everyone points out that I beat cancer once before so why shouldn't I be able to do it again? But in re-reading these old posts I realized how different everything was then. We had so much more hands-on support during my last round with chemo. Plus, I seemed to have more determination, motivation and fighting spirit in me. Back then cancer seemed like a blip on the radar of my life. Now cancer feels like my whole life.

Some things haven't changed between then and now though, like my frustration over parenting during chemo. Just like last time I find myself crying and upset because I don't have the energy to take care of my daughter, have fun with her, play in the snow and come up with creative activities to handle her outbursts (which have been increasing substantially as of late). It sucks. It's not her fault I have cancer. *Why does she have to suffer too?* I try to remind myself that in the big scheme of things I AM a good parent. She WILL be okay. But in the small moments when she won't brush her teeth or go up for her bath and I don't have the energy, patience or mental wherewithal to deal with it, I feel frustrated, sad and sorry for us.

But you know me, I also refuse to remain stuck in the feeling-sorry-for-myself space. If given a choice—and we all have the choice each and every day—I choose to make a conscious effort to live in hope, faith and gratitude instead. Today I chose to get up early to sit with a cup of tea, read my daily meditation books and write a few new affirmations for myself.

The last few weeks have been a real struggle. The new drug I started (Perjeta) did a bit of a whammy on my system—that, plus the accumulation of the other drugs and this horribly cold weather. I've been unable to pull myself out of bed in the morning (despite ten plus hours of sleep) and late getting Miss M to school every day. I've had days where I was glued to the couch, unable to move—literally chilled to the bone and no amount of blankets could warm me—and a whole week with intense stomach cramping, diarrhea, lightheadedness and being short of breath. I've had to cancel appointments and resign myself to letting Miss M watch a full eight hours of television at once.

My oncologist is running some tests to see if these problems are related to something else. If not, and it really is from the new drug, we may hold off on taking it again. She also wants to do another echocardiogram to make sure my heart isn't causing the shortness of breath

I've been having—to be continued. In the meantime, I'm still able to continue with the Herceptin and Taxotere.

Amidst all the medical crap, I continue to reflect on my trip to Europe, wanting to identify the healing properties that I can carry over into my every-day life. It was that trip that rid me of all my physical pain, which has still not returned. That trip brought my cancer tumor marker number to its lowest level since I started chemo (unfortunately, the number has steadily inched back up again since then). That trip was a mini miracle.

I know the biggest lesson is the importance of finding silence each day—silence to just sit, meditate, watch the sunset, pray and clear my mind. In order to do this I recognize I need to ask for help more, let the laundry pile up, leave dishes in the sink, be okay with not going full throttle all the time and focus on me more.

I'm eternally grateful I took that trip to Europe. Travel has always been a source of insight and reflection for me. Maybe that's why I love it so much. It's a chance to get away from the hectic day-to-day and just "be." We all need to do more of that.

That's exactly what my family is doing: tomorrow we leave for Puerto Rico. *Hooray!* We booked the trip earlier in the month but I was awaiting final approval from my doctor—which I received yesterday. So off we go. Looking forward to exploring the island, soaking up the rays, exercising in nature, eating fresh and local fruits and veggies, and of course spending time with hubby and Miss M.

I encourage each of you to carve out some moments of silence for yourself—and just BE.

CHAPTER 8

VISIONS WITH THE LONG ISLAND MEDIUM AND BEYOND

FEBRUARY 12, 2014

Well, it seems that after months of struggling to reclaim my faith and inner warrior spirit I'm finally making some progress. I realize there's no guarantee I'll feel this way tomorrow, next week or next month. For now, I'm a lot happier than I've been in a while.

I've also been receiving messages that I'm on the right track. My tumor markers dropped. My energy levels are good. My pain still hasn't returned. The tumors in my neck have shrunk so much that when I went for a biopsy this week, the doctor could no longer feel where to biopsy. My recent vaginal ultrasound (concerns about me getting my period while in treatment) and echocardiogram both came back fine. I may finally be ready to get off my blood thinners. *Hallelujah!*

Things were further confirmed this past weekend when I went to see the Long Island Medium live in Providence, thanks to the amazing generosity of my Uncle who surprised my Aunt and me with tickets for Christmas. And these weren't just any tickets—our seats were aisle seats mere steps from the stage. You're the best, Uncle M. Thank you from the bottom of my heart.

I love Theresa because she's so unapologetically herself—big hair, crazy nails, glittery four-inch heels, wise-cracking sense of humor, Long Island accent and inappropriateness. She's just who she is—period.

Of course I was praying my mom would come through, but not expecting it in a theater of 3,000 people. So when Theresa ended up standing in front of us passing along messages from my dead mother, I was simultaneously shell-shocked and overcome with emotion. Naturally it was Uncle M's ancestors that brought Theresa to us. They were caught in the deadliest nightclub fire in US history at Cocoanut Grove in Boston. And it was a vision of this fire that sent Theresa our way.

Theresa then acknowledged my mother's presence and first asked if I was in remission. When I said no and told her I was in treatment for Stage 4 cancer, the audience moaned and gasped. Theresa then asked if I was doing holisitic treatment. When I told her yes, she said I needed to continue with that, that she saw tests and numbers confirming that what I'm doing is working.

She said she saw me on the floor at the feet of the Blessed Virgin Mary (which I confirmed by telling her about my recent visit to Fatima, and the audience let out more audible gasps). She told me my mom was there with me on that day and that my mom says it's not my time to join her yet (which are the words I've told my mom since the day I was diagnosed, "Mom, I'm not ready to join you yet.") She also said my mom was sending assurances that I'll be around to celebrate many major milestones in my daughter's life. She used the word "remission" a few times. And before she moved on to the next person, she wished me luck and gave me a big hug (I was the only person that night who got a hug!). It was magical. I left with a renewed sense of hope and faith and confirmation that my mother and the angels are truly watching over me.

I'll try to carry this hope and faith with me even when the days aren't so easy—when my left hand is barely functioning and I can't clip my nails, type, or fish something from my pocket; when my skin is cracked, red, and raw from the endless tearing of my eyes and dripping of my nose that is a side effect of the treatment; and when I don't have the energy to parent the way I want to.

I find myself feeling jealous sometimes of those who have the luxury of sleeping all-day or lounging on the couch after doing chemo. Alas, I know they too have their difficulties. No one is immune.

That's something I continually realize as I chart my path through cancer. We all have our battles to face, our demons, our tragedies and difficult situations with which to contend. Whether it's cancer, homelessness, bankruptcy, divorce, unemployment, infertility—at some point we all reach a crossroads in our life. These challenges shake us to our core. Humble us. Jolt us awake. Then we have the choice to either keep trying to return to what was, or to embrace the change and redefine ourselves and our realities. Each of these moments presents us with the opportunity to make our lives even better than they were before.

Why not seek to live a better life? What have you got to lose?

*Me and Auntie L moments before our amazing
experience with the Long Island Medium*

CHAPTER 9

NEWS AND FINDING THE COURAGE TO SET SAIL

February 24, 2014

Spring is on its way! I can feel it in the air. The birds have returned. The snow is melting. The sun is shining. What a difference it makes in my spirit! I'm feeling renewed—hopeful and full of gratitude.

Last week we had an amazing visit with Auntie Cole who showered us with her playful spirit and love. It always warms my heart to spend time with her. Hubby, Miss M and I seem to be finally settling on a church. We've gone to the same United community church the last three weeks in a row. I've actually been thinking about purchasing a Bible and reading it—a previously incomprehensible thing for me.

The latest news on the cancer front is that we received the biopsy results. I'm glad I went through with the biopsy because it confirmed my suspicions—and the dream I had—that the cancer is different this time around.

Previously my cancer was "triple positive," meaning it tested positive for estrogen, progesterone and HER2. Now, my cancer is still HER2 positive—which is good because two of the three drugs I've been taking are targeted HER2 treatments—BUT, it's no longer hormone positive. This means it no longer feeds on excess estrogen or progesterone—which to me is amazing since I refused all hormone treatment (aka Tamoxifen) and surgery (removing my ovaries)—despite continuous pressure from my Western medicine doctors who thought I was crazy not to as a young 30-something pre-menopausal woman.

I'm so thankful I listened to my intuition.

This also means I have fewer drugs available to treat my cancer, which according to Western medicine is a bad thing. But for me, I wasn't going to take those medications anyway.

Now I'm faced with more decisions. My gut is telling me something I'm not sure I'm ready to hear. The last few days when I've quieted my mind, meditating at the beach, I received the message that I don't have to do chemo.

Of course this goes against conventional wisdom—I know most people will be horrified that I would even consider stopping chemo (which is why I haven't told anyone about this until today). But I know when my intuition speaks I need to consider what it's saying.

The Universe is speaking to me too…

I was guided by my husband's psychic/medium in Europe to read a book by Brandon Bays entitled, "The Journey." In it, the author heals herself from a basketball-sized tumor without conventional treatment, and speaks loud and clear about physical dis-ease being a manifestation of unresolved trauma and disharmony of the spirit and soul.

Then, in the middle of writing this blog I received a call from a new healer I'm working with. She's a medical intuitive who is trained in a number of healing modalities and came highly recommended. She primarily uses muscle testing to tap into what the body/mind/spirit needs and wants. Coincidentally, in the weeks leading up to my session with her, I read an article by Martha Beck in an old Oprah magazine that also talked about muscle testing. What came up in my session, amongst a ton of other stuff, was that chemo may not be the answer.

So where does this leave me?

The question I keep asking myself is, *Am I strong enough to once again go against the grain, against conventional thinking and treatment? Am I strong enough to shield myself from everyone's fear and judgement?*

I listened to my gut when it came to hormonal treatment and my gut proved right. *Why does this seem more difficult?*

I'm scheduled for regular chemo this week and one more dose of the new drug Perjeta next week. Then we've got a PET scan scheduled for the second week of March to see where we're at. I guess my plan is to wait and see the results of the scan and then ultimately make a decision.

As my daily meditation from Simple Abundance said today, *One does not discover new lands without consenting to lose sight of the shore. [So] set the sails. Pull anchor. Cast away... Or stay on the shore. But choose.*

It's so much easier to stay on the shore, stay in the comfort zone, stay stuck. But even that is making a choice.

What will I choose? What will you choose for your life? Can we find the strength to make the choice that feels best to us? And not to everyone else? The choice that honors our truth? The choice that feels right, no matter how scary it may seem?

I feel like I'm getting on the boat, wanting to set sail but still afraid to pull the anchor.

Maybe it's time.

CHAPTER 10

GLEANING PERSEPECTIVE FROM THE LATEST SCAN RESULTS

MARCH 12, 2014

The latest PET scan results are in. The news, as far as I'm concerned, is pretty good.

There are spots of cancer around my left chest, neck, shoulder, armpit and sternum area, which we already knew were there. I can feel them through my skin—now that the lymphedema swelling is going down—but they don't seem to be getting any bigger, which is great.

A few new areas lit up in the bones of my back and shoulder. But the SUV numbers are on the low end and I'm not having any pain. I've had areas on my back light up on prior PET scans and then disappear entirely, or not show up on other scans. So I'm not too concerned about this either.

The other good news is that the two "suspicious" spots from my recent brain MRI did not show up on the PET scan so it would seem the brain is clear. And nothing came up in any of my organs either, which is fantastic.

The only slightly weird thing is the appearance of a pleural effusion around my left lung. A pleural effusion is a build-up of fluid in the tissues between the lung and chest cavity. This fluid could be a bunch of different things. It could be cancer, or not. It could also be from the blockages in my lymph system that prevents my bodily fluids and blood from going where they need to go. Or a result of the chemo or the blood clot I had in my lung. I'm not having any symptoms or pain and my oncologist does not seem overly concerned. For now, I think we'll just watch it.

So that's that.

I also made the decision to stop taking one of the three meds I'm currently on—Taxotere. It is the only chemo med I'm on. I will continue to take the other two meds which are specific treatments for my HER2 positive cancer. They specifically target my cancer cells and don't harm my healthy cells. Some may think it's a gamble to stop one of my meds, but it's a gamble I feel good about. Besides, I can always change my mind.

I have to say that living with the side effects of treatment is a pain in the ass. But it's interesting how the body adapts. With the fingers on my left hand barely functioning and the nails on my right hand about to fall off, I'm surprised at how the everyday stuff still gets done (albeit with way more effort, frustration, pain and time). You realize how much you take for granted—typing, buttoning up your pants, washing a dish, doing your daughter's hair.

The sheer exhaustion I feel most of the time drives me crazy. I want more energy—more energy to be with hubby and Miss M, to live life, travel, be with my favorite people and pursue my dreams. It was great having people here visiting and helping out the last couple weeks. Now that they're gone, I'm struggling again. The housework doesn't get done and making a meal and cleaning up after takes every ounce of energy I have.

But I plug along. Eventually the most important stuff gets taken care of some way or another. At the urging of family and friends, I'm going to inquire about having a home health aide come in to assist with the household stuff and hubby and I are considering asking his parents to come up from Brazil to stay with us for a while, too.

And still I count my blessings and always know it could be worse.

I try to remember what Sylvia Boorstein said: "Life is painful. Suffering is optional." I'm determined not to let cancer run my life, determined to have the most fun I can while I'm here.

On that front, I decided to pursue my dream of becoming a dance and movement therapist. I applied to the summer intensive three-year program for mental health professionals at the 92nd Street YMCA in NYC. I even have a dance audition at the end of the month. Fingers crossed I get in (and yes, my oncologist knows all about it). I'm thrilled at the idea of being able to help other cancer patients heal and process their feelings through music, dance and movement.

Some may say I'm crazy for trying to take on so much while in the midst of treatment, but I say, "Why not?" We all need more fun in life—more passion, stimulation, something to look forward to and live for. Instead of terminal or chronic illness being the end of everything, why not let it be the beginning? Why not use the "free pass" to truly live your life?

Life is too short to sit on the sidelines.

I understand that life is painful, but I refuse the optional suffering.

CHAPTER 11

QUESTIONING IT ALL

APRIL 30, 2014

I t's been a while. I know.

I've been feeling a bit lost, out of sorts, unclear about life, relationships, cancer, treatment and my career.

Sometimes it's hard to still find the joy in life, to not stay permanently stuck in a bad place. It's hard adjusting to a life with ongoing physical pains, depleted energy, a bald head, non-existent sex drive and a left arm that is temporarily out-of-order.

Then last week, as I'm sitting outside struggling to make peace with it all and asking the Universe for guidance, the doorbell rings and it's a special delivery from a friend and fellow breast cancer survivor in NYC. She sent me a gift card for the Metropolitan Opera because she saw "attending the opera" on my bucket list. In that moment, just when I'm feeling at my wit's end—hopeless and losing faith—the Universe sends me this glorious message: to remind me of the beauty in living, the amazing compassion of others, and offering hope, healing and a reminder that God's love is all around.

It's not all bad.

I also received news a few weeks ago that I was accepted into the dance and movement therapy program in NYC. I'm thrilled! The news inspired me to start exercising again for the first time since November.

The problem now, though, is that my left arm and hand are really messed up. Neuropathy has set in. My hand and arm are so bad that I have to type with one hand. I even had to get Miss M to help me open a can yesterday and button my sweater. I can't put jewelry on by myself and I'm having pain at night that runs up and down my left side. *Sigh...*

My body feels so depleted and beaten up. I'm praying I'll be physically well enough come June to do the dance therapy program. I really want this. And I'll be so pissed if cancer takes it away from me.

Thank God my in-laws are coming up from Brazil to help out. They arrive on Miss M's birthday at the end of May and are staying for three months. They're so sweet, helpful, considerate and fun to be around. I'd have them permanently move in with us if they could and I'm psyched Miss M will be forced to brush up on her Portuguese.

This past weekend I went with a friend to my first ever breast cancer conference for women living with metastatic breast cancer. It was pretty fantastic to be in a group of people that can totally relate to my life—where I don't have to explain my bald head or why I can't do a high-five anymore. I learned more about treatment side effects, how to better communicate with those around me about what I'm going through, and why tumor marker tests are not totally reliable, among other things.

I also realized how differently each of us faces and thinks about our diagnosis, treatment decisions and futures—how we can all choose different ways of doing things and end up in the same place. Cancer is such an individual journey. This is something I must remember as I continue on my path. My plan doesn't have to work for anyone else. It just has to work for me.

CHAPTER 12

KEEP ON KEEPING ON

JUNE 17, 2014

I'm back... And my hair's coming back too!

But I ain't gonna sugar-coat it, I'm not feeling too good these days.

They just found another blood clot in my arm. *Enough already!* So back on the blood thinners I go. *Sigh...* My arm has progressively been getting worse and worse. Moving it around is increasingly difficult. My fingers don't move at all now. Living day-to-day with only one functioning hand is taking a while to get used to.

I think what's even worse is the pain—the pain in my fingers, hand, neck, shoulder and back. The pain is there pretty much around-the-clock these days—and it sucks.

While I do have more energy now that I've stopped chemo, it's still not what it used to be. Just going through the regular activities of a normal day exhausts me.

It's difficult adjusting to the limitations of my new reality, the same new reality that forced me to withdraw from the dance therapy program I was supposed to be doing right now in NYC. *Another sigh...* I realized I just didn't have the strength, stamina or mobility to get through the intensive program. Initially, I was pissed. And sad. But it is what it is. I accept it.

Life goes on, and it's not *ALL* bad.

I finally got some awesome voice recognition software for my computer. Now I can just talk into the computer and it types everything for me. It's not perfect, but it sure is easier than typing it all with one hand. At least I still have one good hand! Thank God for that.

Last weekend I got to celebrate the beautiful marriage of my darling cousin to an amazingly kind and talented man. Miss. M was the flower girl, I was a bridesmaid, and the whole event from beginning to end was joyous and full of love. Hubby and I had more fun than we've had in a long time—meeting interesting people, getting tipsy and getting our swerve on—just like old times. I rocked it in heels the whole night!

A few weeks before that Miss M and I spent an amazing week in Ohio visiting our old friends and nourishing our souls. I miss you guys!

We celebrated Miss M's 5th birthday with a fun home-style Brazilian BBQ—complete with my fabulous in-laws. It's so wonderful having their help, love and support for the summer.

And now that summer has arrived, my spirits are boosted by all the lush green trees, beautiful songbirds, beach days and relaxing hours in the hammock with Miss M (that is, when I'm not at medical appointments—but that's a whole other issue).

In terms of treatment, I'm on a break from chemo and pharmaceuticals right now. But I'm doing some new alternative treatments. I started high dose intravenous vitamin C last week. They pump it straight into my port. I actually feel better after, instead of worse. The vitamin C oxygenates my body, boosts my immune system and kills cancer cells. Plus, I keep adding more plant-based cancer fighting elements to my daily routine. I wanted to do hyperbaric oxygen treatment as well, but the cost was absolutely crazy—over $200 a session. And they wanted you to do upwards of five sessions a week. *Are you kidding me?*

I'm also talking to various research hospitals in the northeast about enrolling in clinical trials for a cancer vaccine. I wanted to try a cancer vaccine when I was first diagnosed but they told me because it was still experimental I had to exhaust standard treatment first. So now I'm finally free to try it. I think I found a good one in Philadelphia at the University of Pennsylvania. It's a multi-peptide vaccine with Basilixumab. We're currently going through my medical history to make sure I'm eligible. If I get in I'll be required to make weekly trips to Philadelphia for a while.

In the meantime, I just keep on keeping on. What else is there to do?

I try not to dwell on how crappy I feel. Some days are easier than others. And I notice how much better I feel when I'm having fun, when I have something to look forward to, when I'm spending time with people I love. I know I need to do more of that.

Don't we all?

*Miss M and I at Madison Square Park on a recent
trip to NYC and with the beautiful bride*

CHAPTER 13

CROSSROADS

JULY 14, 2014

Chillin' in Central Park

Not feeling so good these days. My body has taken a turn for the worse and I'm not sure which direction to go next.

In terms of treatment decisions, I need to figure out my next steps quickly. I can feel new tumors growing every week. I have one remaining approved drug combination I can take, Tykerb (a HER2 targeted drug similar to Herceptin and Pertuzamaub), along with the chemo drug Capecitabine (otherwise known as Xeloda). Capecitabine was the one chemo drug my mom tried. It likely contributed to her kidney failure which was the beginning of the end for her. I'm on the fence about taking these drugs but also am realizing that my options are quickly dwindling.

Otherwise, I continue to explore alternative treatments.

Mentally I'm a bit of a hot mess. I spend a lot of time crying. I'm mad I can't be the mom I want to be, that I can't live the life I want to live. I'm trying not to focus on the pain and limitations, trying not to obsess over the fact I may be dying. I'm clinging to the hope contained in messages from the Long Island Medium and other medical intuitives that tell me it's not my time yet. I'm praying for divine intervention, praying for a miracle.

But I have to say, amidst all the pain and sadness, I still manage to have some moments of joy, laughter and peace.

Last week my BFF Auntie Cole came to town and we had two glorious days in NYC with my Cousin J—shopping, people watching, laughing hysterically. This was followed by more quality girl time in Connecticut with my Aunties and their girlfriends. Hubby and I made it out to see a movie and the whole family made it to church last Sunday.

In the end, I know this is what matters most—finding moments of joy and happiness amongst the suffering. It is possible, but some days are easier than others. So please send some prayers and positive energy my way. I need it. I'm at a crossroads.

Fun with Cousin J, Auntie Cole and my Aunties

CHAPTER 14

THE TIDES ARE CHANGING

AUGUST 4, 2014

It's been another rough couple of weeks, but I feel myself finally starting to pull out of the blackness and into a better place. A big part of that has to do with the amazing outpouring of love, prayers, blessings, encouraging words and donations that have come my way since the last post. Thank you everyone! And shout-outs also go to the amazing hands on support of my best friend Auntie Cole who continues to be there for me, my darling hubby, entire family and the special love of the O'Neil crew!

Right after I posted my last blog entry I was hit with a crazy MRSR like infection in my chemo port. It landed me in the hospital for an entire week. Thankfully my family whisked Miss M off to Massachusetts, and hubby was able to take time off from work to be with me and hold my hand as they brought me to surgery to remove the infected port. It's been just over two weeks since I was discharged. I took three weeks of hardcore IV antibiotics and two more weeks of oral antibiotics. I was feeling pretty low, but I think the worst is over.

Last week, I also made the decision to start a new chemo regime—Xeloda & Tykerb. Fortunately they both come in pill form since I no longer have a port for intravenous drugs. It's been exactly one week, and so far the only side effects I've had are nausea and tummy upset. But I also know the side effects of chemo are cumulative.

We also learned that my liver enzymes are elevated, so we need to keep an eye on that. It could be from the onslaught of drugs I just started taking or from the cancer. Time will tell.

Amidst all the craziness, some incredible news came my way. It all started a few years back when friends and family in Massachusetts banded together to create the Graceful Woman Warrior committee to raise funds for my never ending medical expenses. They were scheduled to meet again last week. Now to tell the rest of the story is my fabulous Auntie L:

Ideas had been percolating about what to do— a 5K, raffling an iPad, scheduling a golf tournament. My daughter Jamie suggested I contact The Blowout, a fabulous fundraiser that's been making an incredible difference since 1977. Figuring it was too late, I never reached out.

While Terri was in the hospital, my husband learned that The Blowout didn't have a recipient this year (Coincidence? I THINK NOT!). The brothers O'Neil immediately put Terri's name forward.

I promptly dialed my sister, Dori, and she wasted no time contacting her connections. Fellow committee member, Peggy B, reached out to her brother, a Blowout volunteer since its inception. The serendipitous threads of connection continued all week as news of Terri's remarkable journey and the thousands upon thousands of folks she has inspired reached The Blowout organizers.

I received the call from Dori on the eve of our committee meeting and immediately called Terri.

Tears flowed as I literally "heard" the joy and happiness my incredible niece is forever searching for. Hearing that light, that life, emanating from her being was a gift I will treasure always.

Thanks Auntie L! And thank you to the entire Graceful Woman Warrior committee and the Blowout team. I am so grateful.

Hope to see ya'll there.

Family love

CHAPTER 15

HAPPY DAYS ARE HERE AGAIN

AUGUST 22, 2014

Living with a terminal illness ain't easy. My health really took a nosedive the last few months.

But I've been on the new chemo regime for almost a month now—so far so good. I can feel some of the tumors actually shrinking. My tumor marker number is going back down, I've been able to slow down on the pain meds and I swear my energy level is back on the rise again. Or maybe that's just my spirit being restored…

It seems every time I'm feeling beat down, ready to give up, tired of fighting the fight, the Universe intervenes and brings something or someone my way to turn it around.

Auntie Cole spent much of the last month out here in Connecticut—taking care of me and my family; driving me to appointments; loving me through tears, fears, and frustrations; lifting my spirits and helping me laugh again.

My Massachusetts family continued to rally around me and offered endless amounts of love, support and help with Miss M.

My fabulous neighbors invited us over for meals, brought us fresh veggies from their garden and offered to take Miss M off my hands when I needed a break.

My in-laws spent the entire summer cooking delicious meals, doing laundry, fixing up the house, passing out plenty of hugs and watching Miss M when I had to go to appointments. I can't believe it's almost time for them to go. I'm getting sad just thinking about it.

I think what really gave me the extra boost I needed to start fighting again was being the recipient of The Blowout fundraiser. And it wasn't even about the money that was raised—even though it was VERY much needed and appreciated. The boost came from all the people that were there, the loving energy and fun times that were had by all, the music, laughter, chance to engage with hundreds of fabulous people and to catch up with old friends and make new ones. Being a part of that was extraordinary. I left that weekend feeling energized, blessed, full of gratitude, and feeling my inner warrior come alive again.

So a big thank you to everyone that made The Blowout a reality—the organizers, volunteers, musicians, cooks and servers, face painting team, everyone who donated to the auction, bought tickets, those who came out to celebrate the day with me, and of course, all the family and friends who nominated me and made this year's Blowout one of the best ever! Next year, I plan to return as a volunteer.

And this is how it goes—every time I'm at my lowest, exhausted and ready to give up—the Universe finds a way to lift me back up again, to show me the joy in living and give me the strength I need to continue this journey.

Beyond anything else that I'm doing, I know it's this love that carries me through and keeps me alive.

Three generations of love at The Blowout and girls just want to have fun

CHAPTER 16

ENJOYING THE PASSAGE OF TIME

SEPTEMBER 24, 2014

Family apple picking adventure

This morning on NPR radio they were doing a show about vacations, specifically about America's reluctance to take vacations compared to Europe's support and encouragement of vacation time. What struck me most were the stories from people who called in—the man who worked hard for decades so he could retire early, only to become disabled and unable to do the traveling he once dreamed of or the woman who spoke of her parents postponing travel till retirement and then passing away on their first ever flight out of the country. The message seemed to be—enjoy life now while you can because who knows what tomorrow will bring.

This message hit particularly hard because of the passing of three fellow cancer warriors in the last few weeks—all way too young, all with so much life left to live. Giuseppa Pontearso Robinson, Michelle Pammenter Young and Thomas Hadt, you will never be forgotten.

The beauty is that all three of these people understood the message about enjoying life while you can. They traveled, loved, laughed and made sure to have one heck of a good time.

I realize more and more that's what it's all about. Don't wait. Have your good times now. Take that vacation. Travel. Do what makes you happy.

Oftentimes friends say to me, "I had no idea things were that bad or that you were struggling so much." This is because I try not to focus on all the things that are wrong with me—like the two litres of fluid sitting in my left lung that makes it hard to walk without being out of breath; the constant back pain from the tumors in my spine that make it hard to stand for any length of time; the fact that only one of my hands works; the side effects of the drugs I'm taking that make me nauseous and tired and have me running to the bathroom to throw up and also make my skin dry out and scab up, my fingers full of sores and my eyes constantly tearing so it's hard to see.

I don't want to focus on all the bad stuff. My hair is finally growing back. My pain is much more manageable than it was two months ago. I can still walk. I can still take a vacation and travel. I have many people who love me and many prayers being said on my behalf. As long as I'm still able to get out there and live life, that's what I plan to do. I'd rather spend my time doing that than bitching and moaning.

I'm planning a trip to Vancouver and Bowen Island for Canadian Thanksgiving, a fun girls trip to Chicago to celebrate my 40th birthday in October with Auntie Cole and a trip to Hawaii to visit friends in the New Year. The cancer will just have to take a backseat because I have things to do, people to see and places to go. I've also finally started to write the memoir of my mom's and my journeys through cancer. It's been a long time coming. It feels good to finally get it out of my head and onto the computer screen.

As James Taylor said, "The secret to life is enjoying the passage of time." Words to live by…

CHAPTER 17

LIFE AND DEATH

NOVEMBER 15, 2014

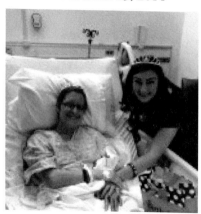

Auntie Cole and I celebrating our 40ᵗʰ

The latest scan results are in. The cancer has spread.

In addition to the cancer in my lymph nodes and around my left breast implant, the cancer has also spread to my sternum, ribs, clavicle, pelvis, vertebrae, spine, neck and into my liver. Plus, I still have liters of fluid surrounding my left lung. It turned out there is a fracture in the left femoral neck which explained the hip pain I'd been having the last three weeks.

I found out this wonderful news in a cab en route from the Chicago airport heading to celebrate my 40th birthday with Auntie Cole and 15 of our closest family and friends. To add insult to injury, as I was getting in the cab I made a wrong move and the fracture in my femur turned into a full break. I arrived at the hotel only to be whisked away in an ambulance moments later to prepare for emergency hip surgery at Northwestern Hospital.

Happy birthday to me!

That was Friday, October 24. I've been in Chicago ever since.

Fortunately, I didn't have to do surgery on my actual birthday. Instead, all the girls came to my hospital room with presents, champagne, cupcakes, good tunes and smiling faces and we managed to celebrate.

The next day I went in for surgery and all seemed well. I had minimal swelling and bruising. Everyone seemed happy with my progress. The pain was excruciating the first few days but that's what pain meds are for, right? Eventually they transferred me to their acute rehab center and I started to learn to walk again.

Unfortunately, more drama lay ahead.

One night I awoke in excruciating pain, finding it difficult to breathe. When the pain didn't go away they sent me back to the emergency room to figure out what was going on. Turns out my gallbladder was inflamed and infected. Fearing my body wouldn't be able to handle another surgery, the doctors installed a drain directly into my gallbladder and started me on antibiotics.

For days I was unable to eat. I felt so weak. We did more scans which further confirmed the presence of cancer in my liver, around my gallbladder and intestines. It felt like the end. All of a sudden, death didn't feel so far away.

Thank God Auntie Cole and Auntie L were here—to hold my hand, listen to the doctors, make plans, distract me with episodes of *Sex and the City*, and to cry endless tears with me.

Thank God for my husband, neighbors and family who kept Miss M's life as normal as possible during this time.

Fortunately, hubby and Miss M managed to make it out here to Chicago for a couple of days. It's so hard being away from them week-after-week. That visit restored all our spirits and gave me the extra oomph I needed to get stronger again. With each passing day, my stomach hurt less and less. I was able to eat more, get out of bed and walk again. But we all knew for the real healing to occur, I needed to get back home to New England.

The great news is that after days and days of back and forth with doctors, social workers, medical facilities and health insurance representatives, it looks like we finally are getting out of Chicago. *Hooray!*

Because of my condition, it is near impossible to get me home on a regular commercial flight. So my fabulous Uncle M found a company called *Angel Med Flight* that will take two guests and me on a direct flight home with an EMT worker and a nurse—everything I might need medically to make it through the journey.

The unfortunate news is the cost of the flight is astronomical. But if my situation truly has become one of life or death, I know I don't want to spend whatever time I have left alone in a Chicago hospital. I need to be home with my family—whatever the cost.

As it stands right now I'm set to leave on a jet plane tomorrow morning. They'll transport me directly from the hospital via ambulance to the airplane, and then from the airport in Connecticut to a rehab facility in Mystic where I'll stay until we figure out what's next.

Ultimately, I would love to go back home again—to be in my house with my daughter, husband, dog and DVR TV shows. But I know I need to build up to that. Right now my body is still weak, my breathing labored, my tummy and gallbladder are still sensitive and my hip still needs a lot more healing, too.

I'll continue to take each day as it comes—to cry when I need to cry, laugh as much as I possibly can, spend time with those I love, try not to get lost in the sadness and despair and to remember there is always hope.

My life is not over yet. But for a moment it sure felt like it was.

CHAPTER 18

A MESSAGE FROM TERRI

DECEMBER 1, 2014

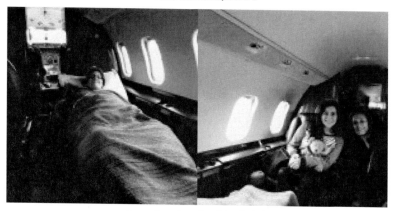

Our miraculous Angel Med Flight

Auntie L here.

My beloved niece has asked me to speak on her behalf. Sitting next to her in Chicago as she painstakingly "wrote" her last post, *LIFE AND DEATH,* was truly a humbling experience. She's been using a voice recognition program for some time and that post took her three hours to complete. I offered numerous times to type for her, but the writing process is a deeply personal experience.

So, I sat next to her, tears flowing, bearing witness to her compelling message.

And now Terri has a new message...

In the end, our Warrior settled into a new "home" at the incredibly loving Weiss Hospice and Palliative Care Unit at Middlesex Hospital. The pure grace, compassion and comfort provided by the staff and volunteers in this exceptional place are truly like no other. Positive energy abounds.

Amidst the inevitable pain and discomfort of Terri's disease.

The rehab we landed in after our miraculous *Angel Med Flight* was only to be a stepping-stone for Terri. Team Terri—as we now call ourselves—were destined to take an incredibly frustrating journey from Mystic to Weiss. Suffice it to say, our medical system is infuriatingly inept at managing the "in between" transition from life to death, but I'll save that dissertation for another day.

After much soul searching, our Warrior chose to move into a space of comfort and love, combined with the best quality of life attainable, in order to embrace and cherish those she loves in her time remaining.

So many things have happened since we moved here a little over a week ago. Within the incredibly heart wrenching emotions of this difficult journey, the pure love is almost indescribable—like the moment I walked into Miss M's classroom to volunteer on her mother's behalf and her face lit up with a kaleidoscope of emotions; or the tears of love and loss her hubby and I shared as we looked ahead at how to carry on Terri's legacy of love for her daughter; a 66th birthday celebration for grandpa from Terri's room, officiated by none other than Miss M; a steady stream of her dearest family and friends, surrounding Terri with light and love accompanied by deeply intimate exchanges; and a Thanksgiving overflowing with gratitude, love, family, music, beauty and sorrow within this end of life journey with our beloved Terri Luanna.

Terri told me that night she felt she was moving closer to dying...

She described it as feeling like she imagines dementia might feel and she said I needed to tell all of you about it.

I asked her what she wanted you to know and she said, "Tell them it isn't scary."

She says it's also a bit confusing and very "busy." There are lots of images, people, dreams and a sort of veil of uncertainty between reality and "something other"—especially while she is sleeping, which she is doing a lot of these days. She wondered out loud if she's "seeing" so much because she's lived and traveled to so many places, and if folks who live in the same place all their lives have a different experience.

She's also having lots of "visitors." After a Reiki session, she turned to me and asked, "Are Daniel's parents passed?"

"Yes," I answered.

"They were just here," she serenely replied.

She told Auntie Cole that same day, that Auntie Cole's father had visited her the night before. He invited her to sit with him on the porch, which is exactly where Auntie Cole spent many cherished moments with her deceased father.

In the end, it was her bodhisattva daughter, Miss M, child of her mother and grandmother, who provided the ultimate gesture of love...

After decorating practically every surface of her mother's room with her stupendous art work and performing dance after dance on Thanksgiving eve (much to her mom and dad's delight), Miss M lovingly whispered in her mother's ear while saying good night, "I'm sorry you have to die, Mamãe."

There were no tears—just a rare moment of enlightenment we can all take a lesson from.

Terri wants you to know she is surrounded—both literally and figuratively—by all of you who love her. She feels your love, compassion and strength each and every day.

She wants to thank each and every one of you who helped bring her "home." She also welcomes your continued prayers, positive energy and support in the days ahead.

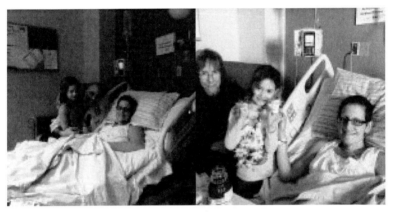

Family

CHAPTER 19

VISIONS

DECEMBER 5, 2014

The sun is rising and our Warrior is sleeping soundly beside me.

It has been a powerful week with our girl. Things have shifted in the last 48 hours. It's uncanny how in the wee hours of the morning, usually between 4:00—5:00 am, Terri and I have the most profoundly intimate interludes.

A few days ago, she looked at me and said, "There're these two Coast Guard guys."

I said, "Tell me about them."

"They're nice… good looking."

"Are they dressed in white?"

"Yes, and they really like the ladies."

"I bet that's my Dad and Uncle Frank. They were in the Merchant Marines. Nana always said they loved the ladies. I think that's your grandfather, Terri."

"Yeah, I bet it is."

I asked her if her mom had come and she said no.

We went on to talk about "home." She said she felt like she had found a new "home." I wholeheartedly agreed, citing the loving, compassionate care she was receiving—reflexology, Reiki and massage at her fingertips, a beautiful room filled with light and lovingly decorated by Miss M, friends and loved ones dropping by.

Auntie Cole and I were up late that night talking and talking. Terri's devoted BFF has not left her side and doesn't plan to. We both wondered what Terri was waiting for, because she was clearly not ready to go.

She told Auntie Cole she wanted to see Miss M, so the next night I shared a magical bedtime hour with Miss M. We sat together at Mamãe's altar, re-enacting how Mamãe sat on her zafu, talking about what meditation is and prayer, about how Mamãe will always be with her. I told her Mamãe wanted to see her, so we made plans to visit her after school the next day. Then we read, "When Someone is Very Sick," a workbook to help children understand end of life.

On the way to the hospital the next day, Miss M furiously worked on a drawing for her "special person who is sick." I asked her to tell me about it. It was Miss M and Mamãe, with vibrant, bright colors, a sun shining and birds flying. Mamãe's dress was particularly beautiful, the bottom filled with flowers. I asked what was at the top.

"An x."

"For love and kisses?"

"Yes, and for God."

Out of the mouths of babes...

Although things had started shifting for Terri—lots of sleeping and glimpses into the other side—Miss M and Mamãe had a lovely visit.

As I danced with Auntie Cole to the "Happy Song" that Miss M played for Mamãe, I caught a glimpse of Terri's arm, gracefully "dancing" in the air—just as her mother's had from her couch the week before she died.

On my way home, I put on my sister Jeanne's Memorial playlist, shed a few tears, but mostly felt numb.

Then, "Will You Still Love Me" came on—that's our "Jeanne song"—the one the five sisters sang to our mother whenever we gathered.

Then it played again… and again… and again. It played continuously for almost 30 minutes until I pulled into my driveway. During that time, I communed with my beloved sister and her daughter, at times raging at the fates and at Jeanne's inability to "save" Terri. But in the end, I pleaded with Jeanne to enfold her daughter in her love.

Things are shifting. Since Miss M's visit Terri has been sleeping mostly. She occasionally asks us things like, "Are the papers ready?" "Does everybody trust everybody else?" She also told Auntie Cole, "It's so beautiful."

Visions are the order of the day.

Together, we are all bearing witness to our Warrior's incredibly courageous journey.

Popsicle "cheers" and Miss M's beautiful drawing

CHAPTER 20

FINAL GIFTS

DECEMBER 8, 2014

Our Warrior gracefully and peacefully journeyed "home" on Friday, December 5th, at 12:41 pm.

Choreographing right up until the moment of her death, Terri Luanna waited for her beloved husband to arrive. Then, as in all she did in her brief life, Terri passed gracefully and in peace, surrounded by all who loved her dearly.

Terri also ensured Miss M was partaking in a fabulous adventure with Auntie L at the time of her death, making sure I was almost home before Papai called to tell me her time was imminent.

I was not destined to be by Terri's side, literally, but rather to "unpack" her leave-taking for Miss M, as Terri and I had done with her mother's cancer journey. The recurring message from our Warrior? Live life fully amidst the pain and suffering.

Papai drove to my home later that afternoon, where he found Miss M and her "favorite cousin," Jamie, listening to pop music and doing artwork between dance moves. Papai took Miss M upstairs to share the news. Soon after, they returned to the kitchen.

Papai then gave Miss M a blue light-up necklace from hospice, beautifully explaining its significance as he peeled off the paper, releasing a bright, iridescent blue glow.

"It will stay blue for three days because that's how long it will take Mamãe to travel to heaven. She will always be with us and will visit us in our dreams."

It was unbelievably heart wrenching to witness, but such an honor to call this incredible family my own. And it was Miss M, child of her mother, who again taught the grown-ups that life does in fact go on.

Within minutes, Miss M asked about the play we were supposed to attend. It was why Miss M and I had journeyed to Dartmouth in the first place—to see her O'Neil cousin, Lauren, make her stage debut.

"Do you still want to go?" I asked.

"Yes!"

Of course, she did. She's her mother's daughter, after all.

As soon as she arrived home, she melted into Papai's arms and went up to bed where he hung their blue light to watch over them while they slept. In the morning, Papai told me he held her close, telling her how much he loved her and how lucky they were to have been loved by Mamãe. Then he kissed her cheek, she kissed his, and together they blew a kiss to Mamãe.

On Saturday, we all gathered in Connecticut—to remember, grieve and celebrate. And Terri continued to scatter her "final gifts"—a red cardinal that appeared outside her friend Patty's kitchen window at 12:45 on Dec. 5th, the perfectly timed "Happy Song" that played three times in the car with Miss M and I as Terri transitioned, and one of my favorites—the dance party Miss M orchestrated, insisting we all dance to Mamãe's favorite, "Empire State of Mind" (aka, New York) sung by Alicia Keys and Jay Z.

Our Warrior will be remembered most for her voracious and passionate love of life, her boundless compassion and her deep and abiding faith in the innate goodness of human kind. The world is a better place because of Terri's legacy of strength, hope and commitment to living life to its fullest. Her indomitable spirit will live on in all of us, the people all over the world whose lives she touched.

Terri had one wish when asked how she wanted us to commemorate her life.

"I want a party and dancing."

Simple as that.

She also wanted her ashes scattered in her beloved NYC, as well as a commemorative bench in Astoria Park. So that's what we're giving her.

In the meantime, please know that together, her treasured army of soldiers who bore witness to, accompanied, and cherished our beloved Warrior, will continue to keep Terri's story and her legacy alive.

EPILOGUE

Terri's story does not end here…

The night before Terri died, she told me she kept dreaming about these scarves. They kept changing colors and would get wet every time she made a questionable moral decision. They were a constant test. Everyone had to wear them. "In the end," she said, "we all have to tie them together until we are all in agreement. It's not about being perfect. It's about being whole. In the end, there is enough love in the Universe for everyone."

How incredibly "Terri" is that? Right up until her death and even beyond, Terri Luanna continues to share her profound visions of hope, universal love and truth, and the critical importance of connection.

From the moment Terri graced this earth, she was destined to teach us all what passion looks, sounds and feels like. Through her fiercely bold narrative, she finds a way into our hearts and leaves a touchstone, an imprint, an enduring legacy that will forever be ours to keep.

Carrying on Terri's legacy has been my lifeline to her. Continuing her blog was literally how I "found my way without her." Ultimately, death is not about saying goodbye, it's about finding new and enduring ways to stay connected. That's what our Graceful Woman Warrior did best—connect. And she encouraged—no she insisted—that we cultivate our connections with ourselves and with each other.

What a gift—to take what we learned from how Terri lived her life and invite it to shape and illuminate the way we go on living ours.

Terri's story lives on—through this book, the blog, and each and every one of you who have born witness to, been inspired by, and/or contributed your own narratives to Terri's, therefore inscribing deeper meaning to hers.

Most importantly, Terri lives on through the magical Miss M, who radiates her essence and her open heart.

One of the last things our Graceful Woman Warrior said to me was, "It meant the world to me to have you all here to celebrate with me. That I was not forgotten."

No, my love, you will never be forgotten. Thank you for welcoming me into your journey—of life, death, parenting, friendship, grief, cancer, seeking, and of the special bond we shared since the day you were born. Your imprint, Terri Luanna, will forever be in my heart.

And in the hearts of each and every one of you...

POSTLUDE

Terri's "Big Idea"

A bold blueprint for a life truly worth living.
Found in her travel journal from her spiritual pilgrimage to Europe.

Why not think big? Dream big?
People may not get you, but the dreamers are the ones who change the world.

When you honor yourself, everyone benefits.

Better to be true to yourself. Be different. Be unique. Honor your truth.

So dance. Love. Pray. Travel. Meditate. Learn. Grow.

Be inspired and inspire others.

Be good to yourself and others.

Find the beauty in life.

Nurture your soul.

The time has come…

Terri Luanna da Silva

Terri's Life Celebration

https://vimeo.com/129388137 PW-terri

"Hymn For Terri"

Composed by Dori Rubbicco

Performed by Tanya Nelson, Dori Rubbicco and Erin Rubico

CODA

MARISA ALEGRIA DA SILVA

12/17/15

(6 yrs. old)

To mom and nana Kanida frum Marisa,

i love 1st grade. My tetchier is Mrss Halland. She is a great tetchier! and I donte gist love Mrss Halland I love you to.

10/25/16

(7 yrs. old)

Dear Mamae,

We will sellabrate your birthday today! We miss you. I am leving you some candy from dylins and a delicous cupcake. It has springkals and your favorite, cocoanut. We also watched vidiows of you and me and papai.

Love: Marisa

12/27/16

(7 yrs. old)

Dear Terri,

I love you so much! I miss you! Sydney moved like a few moths ago. I am at Aunty Laurie's house. Write a letter back! If you don't want me to tell if you send a letter back then I won't. Your wish is my command!

PS-did you have a good chistmas?

10/25/17

(8 yrs. old)

"Reach For The Sky Terri"

Once I fall you help me up

You give me water in a cup

You love me like you do

You know I love you too…

Happy Birthday Mamãe

Love, Marisa

12/5/17

(8 yrs. old)

(Three-year anniversary)

Merry Cristmas Mamãe,

Hi! I miss you! You are still in my heart… even if you died. Well happy holidays! I hope you had a good Cristmas! I love and miss you so mutch!

Love, Marisa

1/3/18

(8 yrs. old)

Dear Mamãe,

I miss you so much. I miss you every day and I love you. And I want you back. You were everything to me. You were the one that made me. I wish you were here making new memories. The old memories are fine with me right now. The most important thing is that I was with you.

ACKNOWLEDGEMENTS

Although the idea of this book was born the day Terri Luanna whispered to me, "I think I'm dying. I want you to tell people," its genesis occurred on November 29, 2014 when Terri called her husband, best friend and me to her hospice bedside. Ever the supreme visionary and determined Warrior she insisted we all, "sign on the dotted 'I give Laurie O'Neil permission to publish my blog' line."

Almost 4 years to the day, we did it my love.

On the 2nd anniversary of Terri's death, I journeyed to Provincetown, Massachusetts accompanied by Terri and her mother, my bodhisattva sister, Jeanne. Since that day, I've been graced with the loving support of so many people whose belief in me helped bring this final version of *Graceful Woman Warrior* home.

To my initial readers and "in house" editorial team: my daughters, Jamie O'Neil and Erin Rubico Ban; best friends and soul sisters, Peggy Barry and Jo-Ann Simmons; beloved sisters, Kathy Rubbicco, Mary Rodericks and Dori Rubbicco; Terri's BFF and forever "411" in times of crisis, Nicole Wademan Dowling; the two most important men in Terri's life—Spider Robinson and Heron da Silva; Peggy Verronneau, Christa Johnson, Maureen Dutra, Amy Dubois, Mary Robinson, Irene Kim, Rani Cruz, Lynn Donohue Dipetta, Kristina Bartlett, Eryka Peskin, Paulette Thomson Clinton, John Barnstead and Stevie McDowell—thank you for saying "yes."

My heart overflows with gratitude for the rest of "Team Terri." Too bountiful to name, I will be forever thankful to the legion of family, friends, health care professionals and blog readers from all over the world who lent Terri unwavering support. Your belief in spreading Terri's message to a wider audience gave me the courage to "pick up my pen."

Deep gratitude to Lauren Mackler, Bernie Siegel and Jean Baird for your time, insights, inspiration and generosity of spirit.

To my son, Andrew, for always "showing up" when Mom needed you.

Thank you, Spider (and Jeanne), for connecting me to the following authors/journalists: Shannon Rupp, James Alan Gardner and Christy Ann Conlin. I am extremely grateful for your guidance in navigating the infinitely complex editorial and publishing landscape.

Much appreciation to Audrey Nathan for the "gifts" of Jill Winitzer and Sue English. I am also very grateful for the keen "eyes" and open-hearted advice of my copy editor, Steve Manchester, proofreader, Mel Stoler and BookBaby adviser, Mike Taylor.

To Terri's treasured cousin, Jeanne Moore, cover designer extraordinaire—you not only validated my instincts and insights, you literally "carried" me through the complex phases of formatting and design. Terri and I are eternally grateful.

Graceful Woman Warrior would not have made it to the finish line without the epic patience, tech savviness and creative brilliance of Erin O'Neil Ban and Jeanne Moore. Infinite gratitude to you both.

Abiding love and gratitude to my darling great-niece and co-author, Miss M. Your passion, dream making and creativity is a constant reminder that your mother is forever in our hearts. I can't wait for our *Graceful Woman Warrior* Dream Book Tour!

Profound gratitude to my mother, our matriarch, Dorothy Rubbicco. Your boundless, unconditional love and zest for life is a shining beacon and inspires me every day to reach for the stars.

And finally, to my cherished husband, Mark. You believed in me before I believed in myself, anchored me through my dream of bringing this book to life, and most importantly, you lovingly "held" me through Jeanne and Terri's journeys and continue to "hold" me through ours.

ABOUT THE AUTHORS

Terri Luanna da Silva was born to two otherworldly, transcendent Canadian artists, Jeanne and Spider Robinson. A self-proclaimed NYC party girl, corporate assistant at Martha Stewart and Oglivy & Mather, social worker, stay-at-home mom, world traveler and writer, Terri was compelled to chronicle her journey with Stage 4 metastatic breast cancer on her blog, *Graceful Woman Warrior.* Using her diagnosis as an opportunity to grow, learn and discover who she truly was, Terri's thought-provoking and transformative narrative captured the hearts and souls of people all over the globe. She was featured on CBC's series, *Living with Fear;* WDTN TV's *Breast Cancer Awareness* series and *Cancer Survivor's Reunite One Year Later;* Living Beyond Breast Cancer's *Let's Talk About It Series;* Healthline's *Stage 4 Breast Cancer: Stories of Survivorship* and *Best Breast Cancer Blogs of 2015;* and appeared in the *Lest We Forget* crawl at the 2015 Hugo Awards Ceremony. Terri's legacy lives on and can be found at www.gracefulwomanwarrior.com.

Laurie O'Neil is a life-long writer who uses the written word as a voice for her life experiences. A Certified Occupational Therapy Assistant and Licensed Independent Clinical Social Worker, Laurie has devoted her 39-year career to empowering, enlightening and engaging others in the critical power of loving connection. Trained by Maria Trozzi from the Boston Medical Center in the Good Grief Program, Laurie specializes in Grief and Loss and Autism. She co-developed The

Caring Tree Family Grief Program, pioneered pro-social/anti-bullying programming in the Dartmouth Public Schools, and is a speaker and activist. Laurie humbly embraces the titles, "Artist of Humanity" and "Love Hero," bestowed upon her by her friend, Dr. Christa Johnson and niece, Miss M, respectively.

Marisa Alegria da Silva is a nine-year-old girl, writing songs, making art, having fun and most importantly eating candy. A fourth-grade student at James M. Quinn School, Marisa dreams of having of having her own horse and all the animals she dreams of. But for now, she can play with her favorite dog, Aura. And to this day, she will be happy, sad, excited, nervous and all those feelings. And her Mamãe will be doing all those things, too. In her memory, she can picture her and Mamãe baking a cake and licking the bowl together. And even though her Mamãe is not alive right now, Marisa knows Mamãe has all those feelings too, and is busy creating beautiful sunsets, putting Marisa's favorite songs on the radio and visiting Marisa by sending a deer or two near her.

READING LIST

Ban Breathnach, "Simple Abundance: A Daybook of Comfort and Joy"

Bays, Brandon, "The Journey"

Beattie Melody, "Journey to the Heart"

Blaylock, Russell L, MD, "Natural Strategies for Cancer Patients"

Block, Keith & Weil, Andrew, MD, "Life Over Cancer; The Block Center Program for Integrative Cancer Treatment"

Boehmer, Tami, "From Incurable to Incredible," "Miracle Survivors: Beating the Odds of Incurable Cancer"

Borysenko, Joan, PhD, "The Power of the Mind to Heal"

Boulden, Jim & Joan, "When Someone Is Very Sick"

Brownlee, Shannon, "Overtreated: Why Too Much Medicine is Making us Sicker and Poorer

Carr, Kris "Crazy Sexy Diet"

Chatfield, Cynthia & Voell, John, "Cancer Report"

Desaulniers, Veronique, MD, "Heal Breast Cancer Naturally"

Franco, Betsy, "Q and A: A Day for Kids; A Three-Year Journal"

Fuhrman, Joel, MD, "Super Immunity"

Hay, Louise L. "Heal Your Body"

Host, Carrie, "Between Me and the River: A Memoir"

Johnson, Christa, MD., "Lynn's Legacy"

LeShan, Lawrence, PhD, "Cancer As A Turning Point"

Miller, Alice, "The Drama of the Gifted Child: The Search for the True Self"

Mooriani, Anita, "Dying To Be Me"

O'Donohue, John, "A Blessing for a Friend, On the Arrival of Illness"

Orenstein, Peggy, "Our Feel-Good War on Breast Cancer"

Rankin, Lissa, "Mind Over Medicine: Scientific Proof That You Can Heal Yourself"

Robinson, Spider, "Callahan's Crosstime Saloon"

Ruben, Gretchen, "The Happiness Project"

Russell Rich, Katherine, "The Red Devil: A Memoir About Beating the Odds"

Siegel, Bernie. "Love, Medicine & Miracles"

Servan-Schreiber, MD, PhD, "Anticancer: A New Way of Life"

Temoshok, Lydia, PhD, & Dreher, Henry, "The Type C Connection: The Behavioral Links to Cancer and Your Health"

RESOURCES/WEBSITES

www.alkalinesisters.com/alkalizing

www.berniesiegelmd.com

www.beyondboobs.org

www.blockmd.com

www.cancer.org

www.cancer.org/treatment/support-programs-and-services/patient-lodging/hope-lodge.html

www.Chrisbeatcancer.com

http://www.ewg.org/foodnews/summary.php

www.foodmatters.com

www.ihatebreastcancer.wordpress.com

www.livingwholy.com

www.mbcnbuzz.wordpress.com

www.neufeldinstitute.org

www.pinkribbongirls.org

www.plantpoweredkitchen.com

www.radiantenergymassage.com

www.replenishpdx.com

www.spiderrobinson.com

MUSIC/FILMS

Rubbicco, Dori, "Hymn For Terri" 2014, www.dorirubbicco.com

- *50/50*
- *Cut Poison Burn*
- *Food Inc.*
- *Food Matters*
- *Forks Over Knives*
- *Hungry for Change*
- *Pink Ribbons, Inc.*
- *Vegucated*